Number SENSE

Simple Effective Number Sense Experiences

Grades 6–8

Alistair McIntosh

Barbara Reys

Robert Reys

DALE SEYMOUR PUBLICATIONS®

Statistics used on pages 76, 79, 80, and 106 are from the U.S. Bureau of the Census, *Statistical Abstract of the United States 1994* (114th edition). Washington, DC, 1994.

Project Editor: Joan Gideon

Production and Manufacturing: Leanne Collins

Illustrative Art: Rachel Gage

Technical Art: Carl Yoshihara

Cover Design: Lynda Banks

Text Design: Nancy Benedict

Published by Dale Seymour Publications®, an imprint of Addison Wesley Longman, Inc.

Order Number DS21803

ISBN 1-57232-264-0

This product is printed on recycled paper

4 5 6 7 8 9 10-ML-02 01 00 99

CONTENTS

INTRODUCTION

Number sense refers to a person's understanding of number concepts, operations, and applications of numbers and operations. It includes the ability and inclination to use this understanding in flexible ways to make mathematical judgments and to develop useful strategies for handling numbers and operations. Number sense results in an expectation that numbers are useful and that mathematics has a certain regularity. A person with good number sense has the ability to use numbers and quantitative methods to communicate, process, and interpret information.

The four-book *Number SENSE: Simple Effective Number Sense Experiences* series is designed to promote thinking and reflection about numbers. The activities help students in primary through middle grades develop number sense through exploring patterns, developing mental-computation skills, understanding different but equivalent representations, establishing benchmarks, recognizing reasonableness, and acquiring estimation skills. Visualization is integral to many activities, as number sense is often developed from visual experiences.

The six sections of this book explore the major components of number sense:

- **Exploring Mental Computation**
  Calculating exact answers mentally, and exploring the thinking that facilitates mental computation

- **Exploring Estimation**
  Working with approximate values to calculate and estimate

- **Exploring Relative Size**
  Developing a sense of the size of a number in relation to other numbers, including benchmarks

- **Exploring Multiple Representation**
  Identifying and using equivalent forms of numbers and expressions

- **Exploring Number Relationships**
  Exploring number patterns and connections between numbers, and understanding the effect of an operation—addition, subtraction, multiplication, division—on two or more numbers

- **Exploring Reasonableness**
  Becoming alert to the reasonableness of a number, solution, or representation, including checks for reasonableness

Each activity falls under one appropriate heading, though most are connected to more than one component of number sense. These interconnections are natural and a reminder that number sense is not a series of disjoint entities but an integration of multidimensional components.

Using the Activities

Each activity is built on the premise that any student can benefit at any time from experiences that encourage them to think about numbers in a sense-making way. The activities can be used in any order, whenever they would be appropriate to anchor, build, and extend students' thinking about numbers in meaningful ways. Most will take from 5 to 15 minutes.

The activities are designed to serve as a source for questions or problems to stimulate thinking and discussion. If the activity is to be presented to the whole class, the activity master may be made into a transparency. Activity masters may also be used to make student copies. When an experience contains more than one activity, begin with the first activity and use the others over a period of time.

Teacher notes explain the intent of each group of activities and suggest ways to present them. The teacher notes contain these components:

- **Number Sense Focus**
  Highlights the main number sense components

- **Number Focus**
  Identifies the types of numbers used in the activity

- **Mathematical Background**
  Describes the rationale or context for the activity, including its connection to different dimensions of number sense—such as relationships of fractions, multiple representation, computational alternatives, and basic facts

- **Using the Activity**
  Offers ideas for preparing students for the activity as well as ways to initiate the experience, questions to raise, and possible directions to take

- **Solutions**
  Provides answers when appropriate and additional insight for some answers

- **Extending the Activity**
  Suggests teacher-directed extensions or variations as well as extensions for students to explore on their own

The Importance of Number Sense

Current reforms in mathematics education emphasize number sense as it typifies the theme of learning mathematics as a sense-making activity. Like common sense, *number sense* is an elusive term that has stimulated discussion among mathematics educators, including classroom teachers, curriculum writers, and researchers. Discussions include lists of essential components of number sense (McIntosh, Reys, and Reys, 1992; Resnick, 1989; Sowder and Schappelle, 1989; Sowder, 1992; Willis, 1990), descriptions of students displaying number sense (or lack thereof) (Howden, 1989; Reys, 1991, 1994), and an in-depth theoretical analysis of number sense from a psychological perspective (Greeno, 1991). Number sense is highly personal. It is related to *what* ideas about number have been established as well as to *how* those ideas were established.

The NCTM *Curriculum and Evaluation Standards* sets forth that children with good number sense have well-understood number meanings, understand multiple interpretations and representations of numbers, recognize the relative and absolute magnitude of numbers, appreciate the effect of operations on numbers, and have developed a system of personal benchmarks.

Number sense exhibits itself in various ways as the learner engages in mathematical thinking. It is an important underlying theme as the learner chooses, develops, and uses computational methods, including written computation, mental computation, calculators, and estimation. The creation and application of algorithms calls upon facets of number sense such as decomposition, recomposition, and understanding number properties. When paper-and-pencil algorithms and calculator algorithms are used, number sense is important as answers are evaluated for reasonableness.

The acquisition of number sense is gradual, beginning long before formal schooling begins. Number sense is often evident at an early age as children try to make sense of numbers. However, growing older does not necessarily ensure either the development or use of even the most primitive notions of number sense. Indeed, although many young children exhibit creative and sometimes efficient strategies for operating with numbers, attention to formal algorithms may actually deter use of informal methods. As students' technical knowledge of mathematics expands, their range of strategies may narrow.

Learned algorithms become the methods most cherished by many students, as they can be executed without much thought. The reaction of a student when asked whether a calculation seems reasonable is often to recalculate—generally using the same method as before—rather than to reflect on the result in light of the context. The lack of a natural inclination to reconsider a calculation is all too common both in and out of school. When selling three items priced at $2.19 each, a clerk reported a total due of $4.88. When the customer responded that the amount seemed too low, the clerk showed no inclination to reflect on the reasonableness of the result. When pressed, the clerk recalculated the amount due. Only when a different total appeared on the register did the clerk recognize an error. While the method of checking (recalculating) is not being questioned, the lack of reflective reasoning is worrisome.

There is evidence that the context in which mathematical problems are encountered influences a student's thinking. For example, while a student may be comfortable in school with a sum of 514 produced by applying a learned algorithm to the computation of $26 + 38$, the same student in a store will likely demand a reexamination if asked to pay $5.14 for two items priced at 26¢ and 38¢.

Students who are highly skilled at paper-and-pencil computations—often the gauge by which mathematics success is measured—may or may not be developing good number sense. When a student reports that $40 - 36 = 16$ or that $\frac{2}{5} + \frac{3}{7} = \frac{5}{12}$, he or she is attempting to apply a learned algorithm but is not reflecting on the reasonableness of the answer. In fact, much of the recent attention to developing number sense is a reaction to overemphasis on computational, algorithmic procedures.

The degree of number sense needed in the world today is greater than ever. Both students and adults encounter a greater range of numbers (government budgets in the trillions of dollars, athletic events timed to the thousandths of a second), in more varied contexts (including graphs and surveys), and encounter more tools (such as computers and calculators) than a generation ago. It might be said that the possession of number sense is the one major attribute that distinguishes human beings from computers. There is every reason to believe that the twenty-first century will demand an even higher level of number sense.

The Teacher's Role in Developing Number Sense

The breadth and depth of students' number sense will grow as they encounter situations that encourage them to reflect on reasonableness, to think about numbers and operations, and to make flexible use of numbers and operations in a variety of situations. Focusing on number sense encourages students to use common sense and to become involved in making sense of numerical situations. *Sense making* is what number sense is all about.

As a teacher, you play a key role in developing your students' number sense by encouraging them to make sense of situations. As activities are explored, spend plenty of time discussing answers and strategies by focusing on questions such as these:

- How did you get your answer?

- Can you explain it another way?

- Did anyone think about it differently?

When there are wrong answers, find out why. Was it faulty reasoning, a computational error, or something else? Sharing how people—including you—thought about the question or problem provides different dimensions of insight into the solution process.

The activities in this book encourage dialogue among students and teachers. We believe that the success of these activities in promoting sense making will be directly related to the quality of the sharing and exchanging of ideas that occurs in your classroom.

References

Greeno, J. G. "Number Sense as Situated Knowing in a Conceptual Domain." *Journal for Research in Mathematics Education* 22 (1991): 170–218.

Howden, H. "Teaching Number Sense." *The Arithmetic Teacher* 36 (1989): 6–11.

McIntosh, A., B. Reys, and R. Reys. "A Proposed Framework for Examining Basic Number Sense." *For the Learning of Mathematics* 12 (1992): 2–8.

National Council of Teachers of Mathematics. *Curriculum and Evaluation Standards for School Mathematics.* Reston, Va.: National Council of Teachers of Mathematics, 1989.

Resnick, L. B. "Defining, Assessing and Teaching Number Sense." In *Establishing Foundations for Research on Number Sense and Related Topics: Report of a Conference,* eds. J. Sowder and B. Schappelle. San Diego, Calif.: San Diego State University, Center for Research in Mathematics and Science Education, 1989.

Reys, B. J., R. Barger, B. Dougherty, J. Hope, L. Lembke, Z. Markovits, A. Parnas, S. Reehm, R. Sturdevant, M. Weber, and M. Bruckheimer. *Developing Number Sense in the Middle Grades,* Reston, Va.: NCTM, 1991.

Reys, B. J. "Promoting Number Sense in Middle Grades." *Mathematics Teaching in the Middle Grades* 1, no. 2 (1994): 114–20.

Sowder, J. T. "Estimation and Number Sense." In *Handbook of Research on Mathematics Teaching and Learning,* ed. D. A. Grouws, 371–89. New York: Macmillan, 1992.

Sowder J. T. and B. P. Schappelle, eds. *Establishing Foundations for Research on Number Sense and Related Topics: Report of a Conference.* San Diego, Calif.: San Diego State University, Center for Research in Mathematics and Science Education, 1989.

Willis, S., ed. *Being Numerate: What Counts?* Hawthorne, Victoria: Australian Council for Educational Research, 1990.

Exploring Mental Computation

Being able to calculate mentally, without the use of external memory aids (including paper and pencil), is a valuable skill. The illustrations demonstrate that doing computations mentally is often easier, quicker, and more appropriate than performing a written algorithm. One of the benefits of mental computation is that it can lead to a better understanding of place value, mathematical operations, and basic number properties. The cassette tape example ($3 \times \$3.99 = 3 \times \$4.00 - 3 \times 1\cent$) demonstrates mental application of the distributive property and involves both operations and basic number properties.

Research shows that students tend to rely on written computational algorithms and do not consider mental computation a viable option—perhaps because they have learned that everything in school must be written. Students need encouragement to develop mental-computation skills and to apply them whenever they are appropriate.

Mental computation lends itself to a variety of thinking strategies. For example, consider these three approaches to calculating how far you can travel on 110 gallons of gas if you get 25 miles to the gallon:

- 25×100 is 2500, plus 250 more is 2750.

- 25×40 is 1000, so 25×120 is 3000, and subtracting 250 is 2750.

- 25×80 is 2000, and 25×30 is 750, so the total is 2750.

As students learn to manipulate numbers in their heads, they develop better number sense and an increased confidence in their mathematical ability. This confidence will encourage them to consider mental computation as an option when straightforward calculations are encountered. Regular opportunities to develop and apply mental computation not only contribute to number sense, but can significantly improve students' ability to think about numbers in a variety of ways.

Postage Stamp Math

Number Sense Focus

- Mental computation
- Number relationships

Number Focus

- Activities 1–3: Whole numbers, decimals

Mathematical Background

The ability to decompose and recompose (that is, break down and build up) numbers in different ways is a valuable number sense skill. Stamps provide a natural model for exploring number relationships, promoting mental computation, and applying the distributive property. For example, to determine the cost of twelve 25¢ stamps, you might reason that ten 25¢ stamps is $2.50 and two more makes $3.00. Written symbolically this is 12 (25) = 10 (25) + 2 (25). Another type of thinking that arises in work with stamps is reasoning, for example, 4 quarters make $1, so 12 quarters make $3. The exploration and discussion of calculation strategies promote number sense.

Using the Activities

1. As a warm-up, ask if any students collect stamps. If so, ask them to share how sheets of stamps are arranged. You might talk about the size of the sheets. Are they a standard size? Do they all have the same number of stamps? The answer to both questions is no.

2. Show the sheet of stamps in Activity 1 for about 10 seconds. Ask students to estimate the value of the sheet of stamps and to explain their answers. For example:

   - "There are 80 stamps, because there are 10 rows and 8 columns. Each is worth 5¢, so the sheet is worth $4."

- "They are worth $5, because there are 10 rows and 10 stamps worth 5¢ in each row."

- "There are 64 stamps worth $3.20, because they make an 8-by-8 square."

- "There are about 100 stamps because it looks like a lot. That's about $5 worth."

The last student used her intuitive notion of 100 to estimate and happened to be lucky. The other students' answers reflected their search for relationships. Regardless of the correctness of their answers, encourage students to build and use mental images.

3. Show the transparency again, and confirm the number of rows and columns. Then, reveal one row or column at a time, and ask students to determine the value of the stamps that are visible and to explain their thinking; for example: "They are worth 50¢ because there are 10 stamps, and I know 10 times 5¢ is 50¢."

4. Mask stamps to reveal certain arrays. For example, show a 4-by-6 array. Encourage different calculations of the total value, such as:

- "4 × 5¢ is 20¢ per row, and there are 6 rows, or $1.20."

- "6 × 5¢ is 30¢ per column, and there are 4 columns, or $1.20."

- "4 × 6 is 24, and 20 × 5¢ is $1, and 4 × 5¢ is 20¢, so it is $1.20."

5. Ask questions to encourage deeper thinking about the numbers, such as:

- If you spend $1, how many stamps will you get?

- If you had only these stamps, how many of them would you need to send a first-class letter to somewhere in the United States? to Canada? to Australia? to Europe?

6. Follow a similar procedure in Activities 2 and 3. Notice that a P stamp is shown in Activity 3. The letter serves as an unknown. When the cost of mailing a letter increases, the postal service issues a stamp with a letter rather than a value printed on it; the letter changes each time rates are increased. Once the new rate is established, the stamp is sold for that value until a stamp with the current cost printed on it is available. You may assign stamp P any value for this activity.

Extending the Activities

- Ask students to inquire at the post office about all the stamp values that are currently available and the number of stamps on a sheet, and to determine the value of the different sheets.

- Have students research how many stamps are in a roll and determine the cost of a roll of first-class stamps.

- Challenge students to research the history of postal-rate increases in the United States. How much did it cost to send a letter via the Pony Express? When did it cost 3¢ to mail a first-class letter? 4¢? 8¢?

Postage Stamp Math

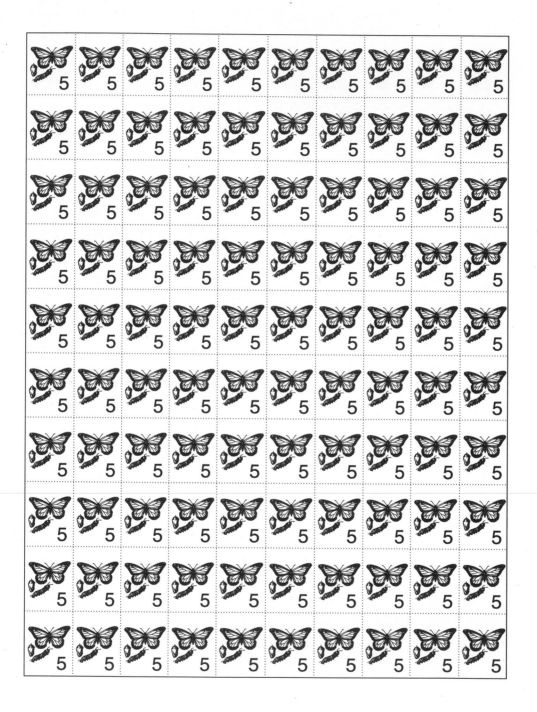

Postage Stamp Math

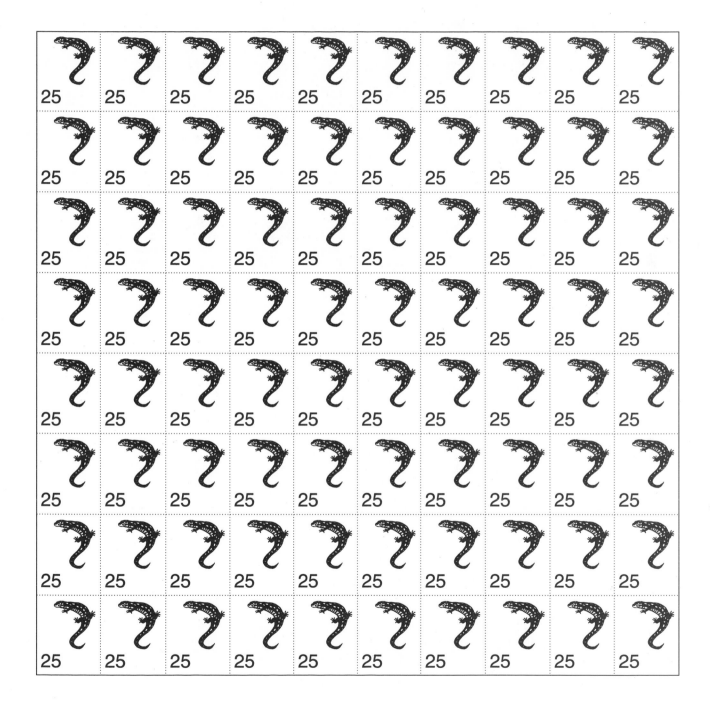

Postage Stamp Math

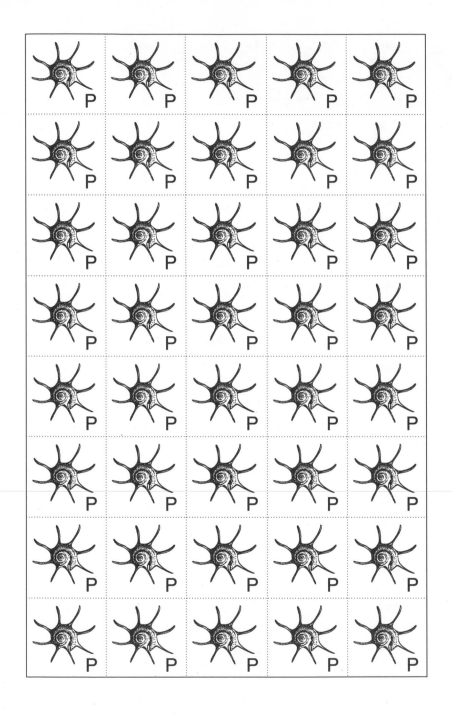

Adding Compatibles

Number Sense Focus

- Mental computation
- Number relationships

Number Focus

- Activity 1: Whole numbers
- Activity 2: Decimals
- Activity 3: Fractions

Mathematical Background

Numbers that are easy to compute mentally and seem to go together naturally are called *compatible numbers*. When computing mentally, it is helpful to recognize and use compatible numbers, such as combinations that total 100 or 1000. For example, when presenting a $1 bill for a 74¢ purchase, knowing compatible numbers helps the buyer compute the correct change (74¢ + 26¢ = $1). Helping students recognize and use compatible numbers encourages them to think about numbers and to look for relationships among them.

Using the Activities

1. Show the first box of numbers in Activity 1. Ask students to find pairs of numbers that total 100 and to explain how they found each pair. Which pairs were easiest to find? Which were hardest to find? Why?

2. For the second box of numbers, ask students to find pairs that total 1000. Encourage discussion.

3. In Activity 2, show the $1 bill. Ask one student to name a purchase price less than 100¢ ($1.00) and ask another to name the amount of change that would be received. Do this several times, and ask that participants share their thinking. Repeat the procedure for the $20 and the $100 bill. For example: An item costs $39.95. What change will you get?

4. When all three bills have been revealed, continue the activity. Have one student name a cost for an item (such as 36¢ or $18.95) and another state the change from the appropriate bill.

5. In Activity 3, ask students to find pairs of fractions that total 1 and to explain their thinking. Which pairs were easiest to find? Which were hardest? Why?

6. Place two pencils on the pizza illustration to indicate a slice of pizza. Ask students to estimate what fraction of the pizza the slice is and the amount of pizza remaining. After a few fractions have been named, you might ask students to draw a circle on a piece of paper, cut out a "slice" of their "pizza," and name the fraction of the pizza in the piece and the amount of pizza remaining. *Precision is not critical; the complementary relationship between the piece and the remaining part is. If one student estimates a piece to be $\frac{1}{6}$, then $\frac{5}{6}$ of the pizza is left; if another student estimates the same piece to be $\frac{1}{7}$, then $\frac{6}{7}$ is left.*

Extending the Activities

- Ask students to list as many number pairs that total 100 (or 20 or 1) as possible in 1 minute.

- Put students into pairs, and have one student name a number between 0 and 10 (or between 0 and 100), and have the partner name its pair so that the total is 10 (or 100).

- In Activity 3, ask students which three fractions are the largest (or smallest). Have them explain how they decided, and discuss the relationships or patterns they see.

Adding Compatibles

Find pairs of numbers that total 100.

25	82	65	8	14
37	21	88	51	30
86	92	35	18	75
70	49	12	79	63

Find pairs of numbers that total 1000.

450	700	810	501	950
250	650	125	222	305
50	499	190	300	550
695	778	875	350	750

Adding Compatibles

Adding Compatibles

Find pairs of fractions that total 1. Use the pizza to show a fraction; then name the compatible fraction.

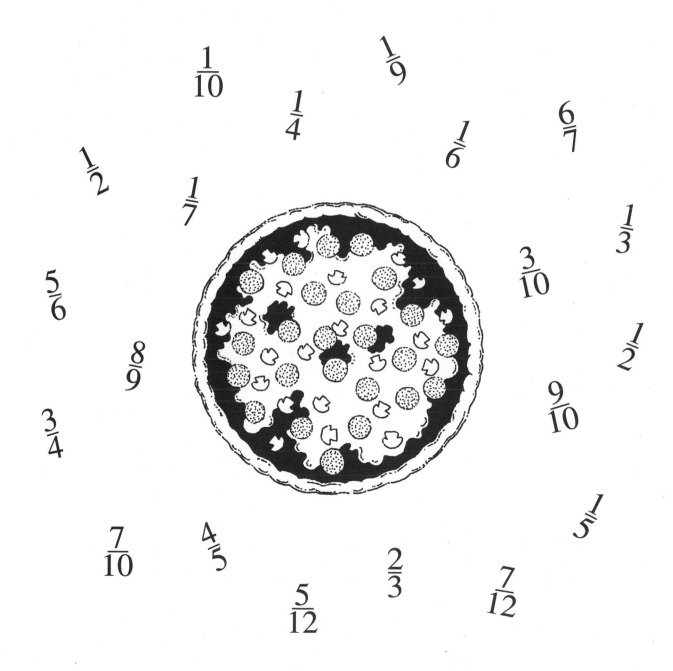

$\frac{1}{10}$ $\frac{1}{9}$ $\frac{1}{4}$ $\frac{6}{7}$

$\frac{1}{6}$

$\frac{1}{2}$ $\frac{1}{7}$ $\frac{1}{3}$

$\frac{3}{10}$

$\frac{5}{6}$ $\frac{1}{2}$

$\frac{8}{9}$ $\frac{9}{10}$

$\frac{3}{4}$

$\frac{1}{5}$

$\frac{7}{10}$ $\frac{4}{5}$ $\frac{2}{3}$ $\frac{7}{12}$

$\frac{5}{12}$

EXPERIENCE 3

Dollars and Percents

Number Sense Focus

- Mental computation
- Multiple representation
- Relative size

Number Focus

- Activities 1–2: Fractions, percents

Mathematical Background

Percent is based on 100, and so is the dollar. Our monetary system provides many opportunities to connect ratio and percent in mathematically meaningful and challenging ways.

Using the Activities

These activities provide the visual stimulus for encouraging students to think about and explore relationships among coins and bills.

1. In Activity 1, ask students to name something they could buy with the money shown. Then, ask questions about the relationships between the coins and bills. For example:

    - Find a coin that is $\frac{1}{2}$ (or 50%) the value of another coin.

    - Find a bill that is twice the value of a coin.

    - Choose any two pieces of money. What percent is one of the other? What fraction is one of the other?

2. Activity 2 allows you to extend your questions to other bills as well.

    - Find a bill that is $\frac{1}{2}$ (or 50%) the value of another bill.

    - Find a bill that is four times the value of a coin.

- Choose any two bills. What percent is one bill of the other? What fraction is one bill of the other?

- Choose two bills so that one is 50% of the other. So that one is 25% of the other. So that one is 5% of the other.

- Choose any coin and any bill so that one is 50% of the other. So that one is 5% of the other. So that one is 1% of the other. So that one is less than 1% of the other.

Extending the Activities

- Have students research the history of coins in the United States. For example, when and where was the first dime minted?

- Ask students to explore another country's currency—the denominations of coins and bills, and how much they will buy (their exchange rate).

- Ask students to bring in currency from other countries. They can compare symbols and images and research the current exchange rate of each currency.

Dollars and Percents

Dollars and Percents

EXPERIENCE 4

Will You Do It in Your Head?

Number Sense Focus

- Mental computation
- Number relationships

Number Focus

- Activities 1 and 5: Whole numbers
- Activity 2: Fractions
- Activity 3: Decimals
- Activity 4: Percents

Mathematical Background

Research shows that middle-grades and junior-high students often apply written algorithms to computations that would be more efficient to do mentally. This reliance on pencil and paper probably reflects the emphasis given to written computation in school. Calculators are a powerful computational tool, but sensible use of them should be encouraged. We should not automatically use a calculator any more than we should automatically use written algorithms.

Using the Activities

These activities encourage students to think about doing computations mentally and to reflect on appropriate computational alternatives.

1. In each activity, reveal the illustration at the top. Ask students for other ways to do the computation, and talk about the strategies they suggest. Survey students about which methods they prefer, and encourage them to explain their choices; the sharing of their explanations is the heart of these activities.

2. One at a time, reveal the computations. Ask students whether each calculation can be performed mentally with ease, whether it is very difficult, or in between—possible but requiring thought. Make a list of the

"easy" problems. Students rarely agree on what is easy, which makes for great discussions—and reminds everyone that people often see the same problem quite differently. Encourage students to explain why they find a particular computation easy. Students sometimes think a computation is easy when it isn't. For example, in Activity 2, some students may compute $\frac{3}{7} + \frac{2}{3}$ as $\frac{5}{10}$ and report that it is easy. Observations like this offer natural opportunities for follow-up.

3. Ask students which computation in the set is the hardest for them to do mentally, and discuss their choices.

4. Focus attention on the idea that the numbers and operations determine the mental computational difficulty. In Activity 1, 48 + 51 lends itself to mental computation. On the other hand, it is difficult to compute 48×51 mentally, but easy to estimate if we think about 50×50. In Activity 5, two of the computations become easy as soon as zero is recognized as a factor.

Extending the Activities

● ●

- Ask students to make up a new computation that is easy to do mentally. Ask them to explain why it is easy.

- Ask for another computation that is difficult to do mentally, and ask students to explain why it is difficult.

Will You Do It in Your Head?

Which of these problems are:

Easy for you to do in your head?

Possible for you to do in your head but need extra thought?

Too difficult to do in your head? Why?

1. 15×40

2. 34×100

3. 7×400

4. 19×27

5. $450 \div 45$

6. $399 \div 3$

7. 600×600

8. 25×480

9. $15 \times 7 \times 2$

10. $24 \times 5 \times 2$

11. $48 + 51$

12. 48×51

Will You Do It in Your Head?

Which of these problems are:

Easy for you to do in your head?

Possible for you to do in your head but need extra thought?

Too difficult to do in your head? Why?

1. $\dfrac{1}{5} + \dfrac{1}{6}$ 2. $\dfrac{3}{4} + \dfrac{3}{4}$

3. $\dfrac{1}{4} + \dfrac{1}{8}$ 4. $1 - \dfrac{2}{3}$

5. $1\dfrac{1}{2} - \dfrac{3}{4}$ 6. $\dfrac{1}{2} - \dfrac{1}{3}$

7. $2 - \dfrac{3}{4}$ 8. $\dfrac{3}{7} + \dfrac{2}{3}$

9. $1\dfrac{1}{2} + 2\dfrac{3}{4}$ 10. $\dfrac{1}{2} \times 18$

11. $3 \div 4$ 12. $1 \div \dfrac{1}{8}$

Will You Do It in Your Head?

Which of these problems are:

Easy for you to do in your head?

Possible for you to do in your head but need extra thought?

Too difficult to do in your head? Why?

1. $1 - 0.045$

2. $0.5 - 0.25$

3. 0.1×87

4. 0.25×12

5. $0.632 - 0.5$

6. $1.001 - 0.45$

7. 0.01×450

8. $52 \div 0.1$

9. $8 \div 0.5$

10. $376 \div 0.001$

11. 400×0.5

12. $3 \div 0.25$

Will You Do It in Your Head?

Which of these problems are:

Easy for you to do in your head?

Possible for you to do in your head but need extra thought?

Too difficult to do in your head? Why?

1. 10% of $18

2. 50% of 48

3. 5% of 90

4. 1% of $600

5. 25% of $480

6. 0.1% of $600

7. 99% of 75

8. 10% of 450

9. 15% of $40

10. 75% of $60

11. $33\frac{1}{3}$% of $15

12. $66\frac{2}{3}$% of 45

Will You Do It in Your Head?

Which of these problems are:
   Easy for you to do in your head?
   Possible for you to do in your head but need extra thought?
   Too difficult to do in your head? Why?

1. $25 \times 13 \times 4$

2. $\dfrac{840 + 160}{40}$

3. $17 \times 2 \times 5 \times 20$

4. $86 \times 5 \times 17 \times 0$

5. $48 \times 50 \times 20 \div 6 \times 4$

6. $56 \times 4 \times 5 \times 5$

7. $\dfrac{25 \times 36 \times 16}{12 \times 3}$

8. $\dfrac{18 \times 35 \times 6 \times 0 \times 5 \times 2}{18}$

9. $40 \times 500 \times 49 \times 6 \div 42$

10. $25 \times 25 \times 25 \times 25 \times 8 \div 25 \times 25$

Sorting Products

Number Sense Focus

- Mental computation
- Estimation
- Relative size

Number Focus

- Activities 1–3: Decimals

Mathematical Background

Being able to mentally compute products involving decimals, and to recognize how a product is affected when one factor is between 0 and 1, are useful number sense skills. Once a product has been computed, it becomes important to think about the relative size of the answer.

Using the Activities

These activities combine mental computation and the ordering of numbers by relative size, with a focus on products in which one factor is between 0 and 1.

1. As a warm-up, copy this illustration onto the board:

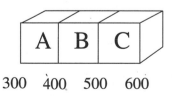

300   400   500   600

Explain that the drawing shows boxes for sorting numbers. Numbers between 300 and 400 go into Box A. Ask students to name several numbers that belong in each box. What is the largest number that can be placed in Box B? the smallest number? These questions address what to do with values falling on a boundary, such as 400. Different answers can be defended; the important issue is to decide on a plan for handling boundary values.

2. Make a copy of each activity for the students, or ask them to draw lines on a piece of paper (such as __ __ __ __ __ __ __ __ __), where the number of lines equals the number of boxes shown. In each activity, ask students to decide which product goes where and to write the correct letter in the box.

3. Have students describe how they solved the puzzles, and encourage a variety of explanations.

Solutions

Activity 1	Activity 2	Activity 3
1. PERFECT	1. BE HAPPY	1. SMILE TODAY
2. EXCELLENT	2. GREAT JOB	2. YOU DID IT

Extending the Activities

• •

- Ask students to propose other computations that belong in a particular box.

- Challenge students to make up computation problems that have a result between certain values—such as 500 to 600; 5000 to 6000; or 50,000 to 60,000—and to explain how they constructed their problems.

- Give students an opportunity to construct a series of mental computations that will reveal a secret message.

Sorting Products

1. Decide in which box each letter should be placed.
   Explain your decisions.

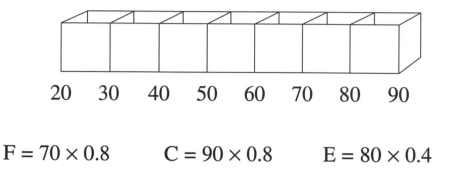

   20   30   40   50   60   70   80   90

   $F = 70 \times 0.8$ $C = 90 \times 0.8$ $E = 80 \times 0.4$ $T = 0.87 \times 100$

   $R = 70 \times 0.6$ $P = 0.7 \times 40$ $E = 0.5 \times 130$

   What is the message?

2. Decide in which box each letter should be placed.
   Explain your decisions.

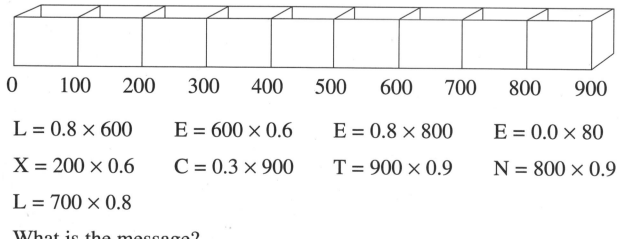

   0   100   200   300   400   500   600   700   800   900

   $L = 0.8 \times 600$ $E = 600 \times 0.6$ $E = 0.8 \times 800$ $E = 0.0 \times 80$

   $X = 200 \times 0.6$ $C = 0.3 \times 900$ $T = 900 \times 0.9$ $N = 800 \times 0.9$

   $L = 700 \times 0.8$

   What is the message?

Sorting Products

1. Decide in which box each letter should be placed.
   Explain your decisions.

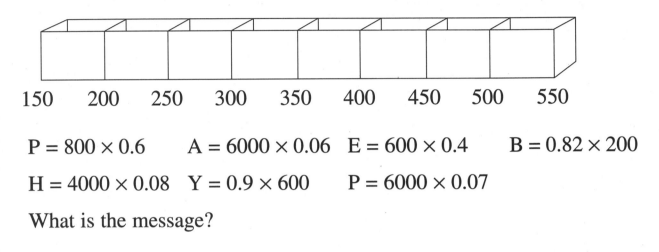

150   200   250   300   350   400   450   500   550

$P = 800 \times 0.6$ $\qquad$ $A = 6000 \times 0.06$ $\quad$ $E = 600 \times 0.4$ $\qquad$ $B = 0.82 \times 200$

$H = 4000 \times 0.08$ $\quad$ $Y = 0.9 \times 600$ $\qquad$ $P = 6000 \times 0.07$

What is the message?

2. Decide in which box each letter should be placed.
   Explain your decisions.

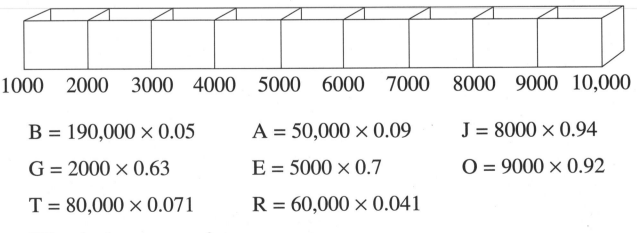

1000   2000   3000   4000   5000   6000   7000   8000   9000   10,000

$B = 190,000 \times 0.05$ $\qquad$ $A = 50,000 \times 0.09$ $\qquad$ $J = 8000 \times 0.94$

$G = 2000 \times 0.63$ $\qquad$ $E = 5000 \times 0.7$ $\qquad$ $O = 9000 \times 0.92$

$T = 80,000 \times 0.071$ $\qquad$ $R = 60,000 \times 0.041$

What is the message?

Sorting Products

1. Decide in which box each letter should be placed.
   Explain your decisions.

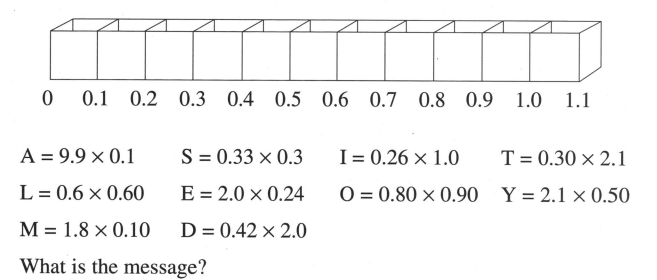

0   0.1   0.2   0.3   0.4   0.5   0.6   0.7   0.8   0.9   1.0   1.1

A = 9.9 × 0.1   S = 0.33 × 0.3   I = 0.26 × 1.0   T = 0.30 × 2.1

L = 0.6 × 0.60   E = 2.0 × 0.24   O = 0.80 × 0.90   Y = 2.1 × 0.50

M = 1.8 × 0.10   D = 0.42 × 2.0

What is the message?

2. Decide in which box each letter should be placed.
   Explain your decisions.

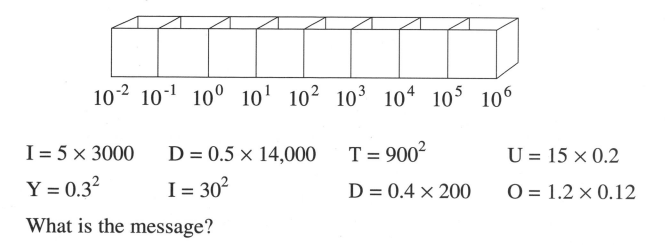

10^{-2} 10^{-1} 10^{0} 10^{1} 10^{2} 10^{3} 10^{4} 10^{5} 10^{6}

I = 5 × 3000   D = 0.5 × 14,000   T = 900^2 U = 15 × 0.2

Y = 0.3^2 I = 30^2 D = 0.4 × 200   O = 1.2 × 0.12

What is the message?

EXPERIENCE 6

• •

Choose Your Path

Number Sense Focus

• Mental computation

Number Focus

• Activities 1, 3–5: Whole numbers
• Activity 2: Whole numbers, fractions

Mathematical Background

• •

Mental computation helps us to think about numbers, to recognize numbers that are easy to compute, to apply mathematical properties, and to explore relationships. For example:

• $2 + 5 \times 3$ produces a different result from $(2 + 5) \times 3$.

• A factor of 0 always produces a product of 0.

• $5 \times 5 \times 4$ is easy to compute mentally.

These activities provide opportunities to practice mental computation in an engaging and challenging context.

Using the Activities

• •

You may want to distribute a copy of the mazes to each student so they can record their thinking.

1. Explain the rules for moving through the maze:

    • Begin at the left, and work your way to the right.

    • You must always move to the right, and you cannot retrace the same path.

    • Begin at the Start Number, and use each result in the next step.

2. In Activity 1, make sure students realize that everyone is to begin with the same Start Number, 10. Have each student trace a path, find its result, and then write the result along with their name on the board. Ask students not to reveal their paths, but simply to make a list of their results:

Anna   5000
Ben   5000
Carlin   1400

As the list grows, you might challenge students to find one of the paths on the list. Although Ben and Anna got the same result, they could have traveled different paths.

Anna could have found $[(10 + 50) \times 40 - 400] \times 3 - 1000 = 5000$, while Ben found $[(10 \times 40 + 50) \times 2 + 100] \times 5 = 5000$.

3. You might ask one student to trace a path at the overhead while another writes the resulting expression. (Be sure students understand the order of operations and correctly use grouping symbols when they are needed.) Ask students which paths produce the greatest value after two steps and which give a result of zero. Then, have them answer the other questions about the maze.

4. Follow a similar procedure for Activities 2 and 3.

5. The blank mazes in Activities 4 and 5 can be used for students to create their own mazes.

    • Provide a Start Number, and have students fill in a value and operation for each line.

    • Let the student provide a Start Number and have students fill in the values and operations. Students can make a simple maze as well as a tough maze.

    As students share a variety of answers, everyone will be exposed to the idea that there are many possible solutions.

Solutions

Activity 1

1. Answers will vary.
2. Possible answer: $[(10 - 5) \times 80 \times 5 - 1000\ ] \times 5 = 5000$
3. $[(10 - 5) \times 200 + 1500] \times 400 - 1000 = 999{,}000$
4. $[(10 + 50) \times 2 \times 5 - 1000] \times 5 = {}^-2000$

Activity 2

1. Answers will vary.
2. Possible answer: $50 \div \frac{1}{2} \div \frac{1}{4} \div 10 \times 5 + 400 = 600$
3. $50 \times 2 \times 30 \div 25 \times 5 \times 6 = 3600$
4. Possible answer: $50 \div \frac{1}{2} \div \frac{1}{4} \times 0 \times 5 \times 6 = 0$

Activity 3

1. Answers will vary.
2. Possible answer: $2 \times 10 \times 4 \div 8 + 100 = 110$
3. $2 \times 10 \times 4 \times 40 \times 3 + 800 = 10{,}400$
4. $(2 \times 20 \times 1 - 200) \times 10 \times 3 = {}^{-}4800$
   ($2 \times 20 \div 40 \times 10 \times 3 = 30$ is the smallest positive finish number.)

Extending the Activities

• •

- Ask students to change the Start Number and observe how the results change.

- Indicate a particular maze, and ask students whether they can change one operation at a particular step to produce a greater result than any found so far, which operation it would be, and why it would work.

- Challenge students to create their own mazes.

Choose Your Path

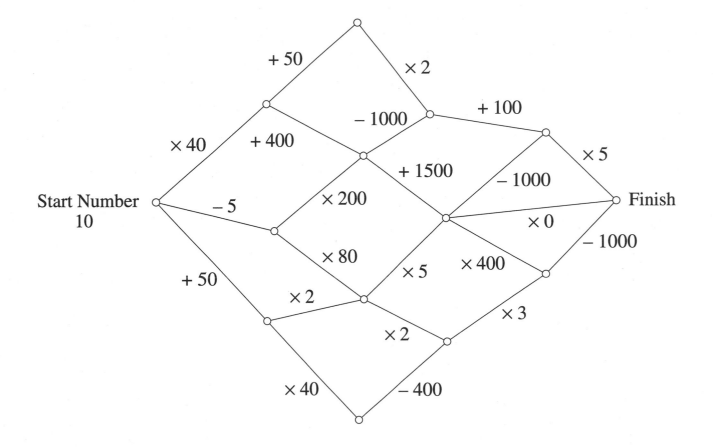

1. Trace three different paths, and find the result of each path.

2. Find a path with a result of 5000.

3. Which path has the greatest result?

4. Which path has the least result?

Choose Your Path

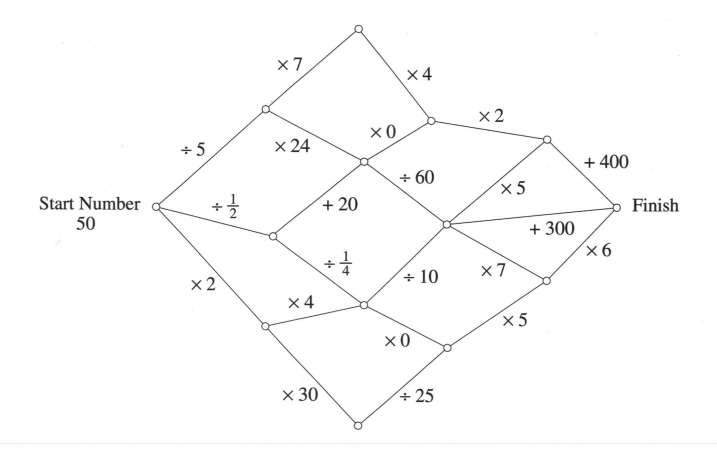

1. Trace three different paths, and find the result of each path.

2. Find a path with a result of 600.

3. Which path has the greatest result?

4. Which path has the least result?

Choose Your Path

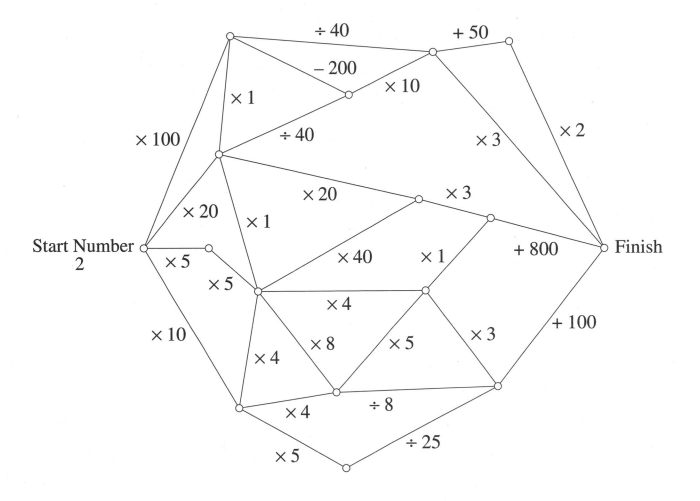

1. Trace three different paths, and find the result of each path.

2. Find a path with a result of 110.

3. Which path has the greatest result?

4. Which path has the least result?

Choose Your Path

Start Number _____

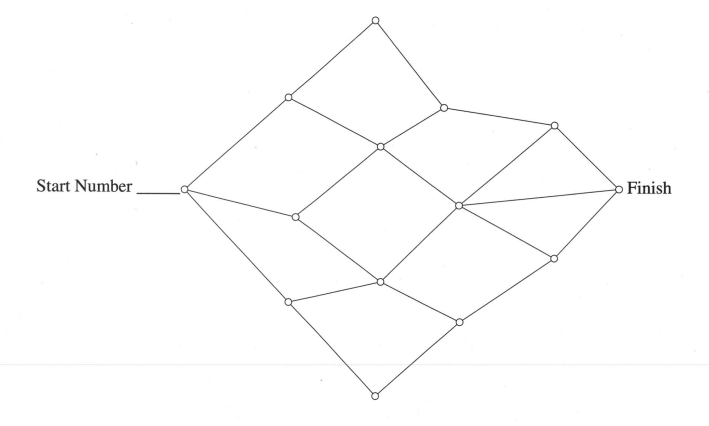

Finish

Choose your Start Number. Enter values and operations, then find the result of each path.

Choose Your Path

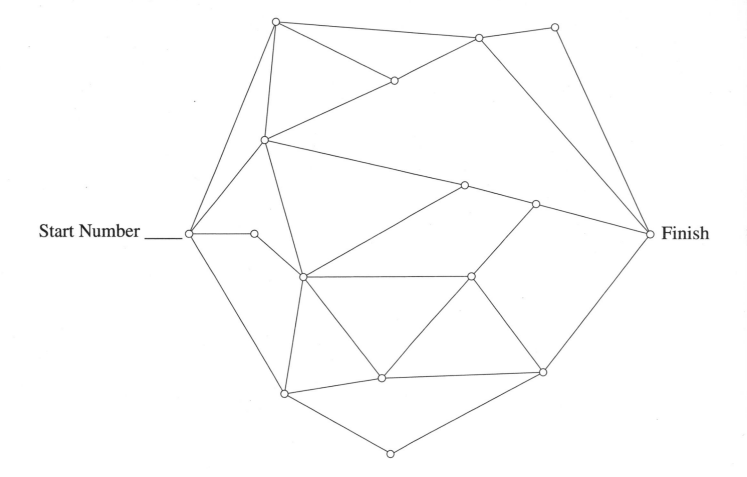

Start Number _____

Finish

Choose your Start Number. Enter values and operations, then find the result of each path.

EXPERIENCE 7

More Choose Your Path

Number Sense Focus

- Mental computation
- Estimation

Number Focus

- Activities 1–3: Decimals

Mathematical Background

Multiplying and dividing by numbers between 0 and 1 produce results that often surprise students. For example, multiplying a positive number by a number between 0 and 1 gives a product that is less than the first factor. This result conflicts with many prior experiences students have had with multiplication in which the product was greater than the first factor. Estimation can play a powerful role in predicting the results of such computations.

Using the Activities

The numbers in this activity have been selected to encourage mental computation.

1. Explain the rules for moving through the maze:

    - Begin at the left, and work your way to the right.
    - You must always move to the right, and you cannot retrace the same path.
    - Begin at the Start Number, and use each result in the next step.

2. In Activity 1, make sure students understand that everyone is to begin at the left with the same Start Number, 100. Have each student trace a path, find its result, and write the result and their name on the board. For example:

Ashley	10	Byron	1000
Cain	1	Su	10,000

As the list grows, you might challenge students to find one of the paths on the list.

3. You might ask one student to trace a path at the overhead while another writes the resulting expression. Ask students which paths produce the greatest value after two or three steps. Then, have them answer the other questions about the maze.

4. Follow a similar procedure for Activities 2 and 3. If your students don't have enough experience with mental computations of this type, you may want to make calculators available. In Activity 3, check whether students realize that moving along the top and bottom boundaries of the maze produce identical results at each step. This provides a nice connection between multiplication and division of decimals.

Solutions

Activity 1

1. 10,000
2. 1000
3. Possible answer: $100 \times 100 \div 0.1 \times 10 \times 0.1 \div 0.01 = 10,000,000$
4. $100 \times 1 \div 0.1 \times 0.01 \times 100 \div 100 = 10$

Activity 2

1. Answers will vary.
2. $(100 \div 0.25 - 100) \div 0.1 \times 0.5 \div 0.5 = 3000$
3. Possible answer: $100 \div 0.25 \times 0.5 \div 0.5 \times 3 \div 0.2 = 6000$
4. $(100 \times 0.1 - 10) \times 500 \times 0.5 \div 0.5 = 0$

Activity 3

1. Answers will vary.
2. $5 \div 0.25 \times 0.5 \times 0.3 \times 0.25 = \frac{3}{4}$
3. Either outside path will produce 2000, the largest result.
4. Any path with 0 as a product will have a result of 0.

Extending the Activities

● ●

- Indicate a maze, and ask students: If you could change one operation at one step to produce the largest result, which operation would it be? Why?

- Challenge students to create their own mazes.

More Choose Your Path

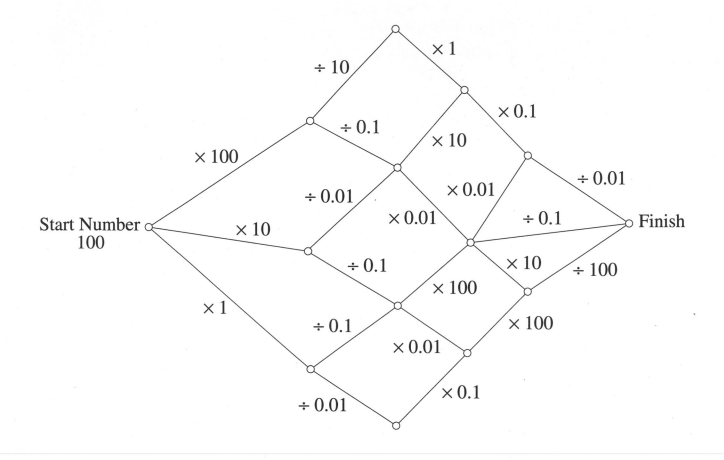

1. Keep to the top path. What is the result?

2. Keep to the bottom path. What is the result?

3. Which path has the greatest result?

4. Which path has the least result?

More Choose Your Path

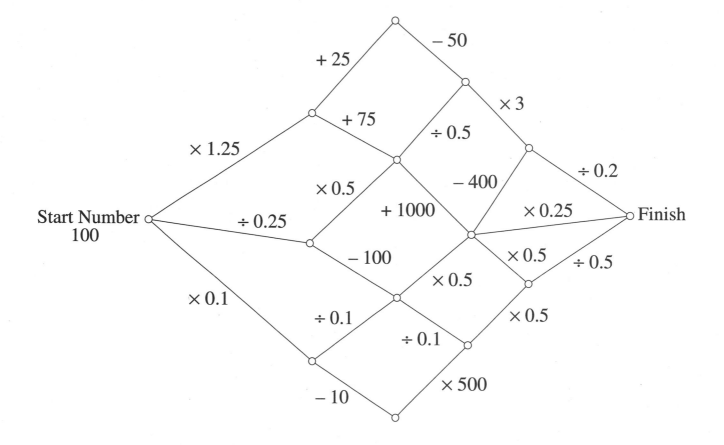

1. Trace three different paths, and find the result of each path.

2. Find a path with a result of 3000.

3. Which path has the greatest result?

4. Which path will give a result of 0?

More Choose Your Path

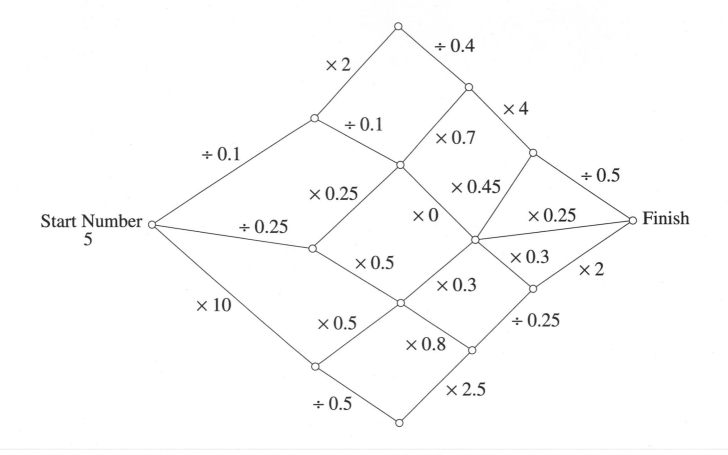

1. Trace three different paths, and find the result of each path.

2. Find a path with a result of $\frac{3}{4}$.

3. Which path has the greatest result?

4. Which path has the least result?

Exploring Estimation

Estimates are useful when exact answers are impossible, unrealistic, or unnecessary. Measurements such as length, area, capacity, volume, distance, and time are approximations; they can be made more accurate by using a smaller unit, but they are always approximate. Estimation is about producing answers that are close enough to allow for good decisions without making extremely precise measurements or doing elaborate, exact computations.

The first step in developing estimation skill is to learn to recognize whether a particular situation requires an exact answer or an estimate, and the degree of accuracy needed. When timing a slow-cooking casserole, half an hour more or less may not be crucial; when using a microwave, seconds matter. Deciding whether to estimate and how closely to estimate encourages, promotes, and rewards high-level mathematical thinking.

Estimation strategies are quite different from those we employ when an exact answer is needed. One valuable estimation technique is relating the estimate to a referent, or benchmark, that we know—such as the height of one story of a building or the capacity of a milk carton. People with good number sense use a variety of personal benchmarks.

Research has shown that estimation employs mental computation, rewards flexible thinking, challenges students to think about numbers in ways that are meaningful for them, develops an awareness of multiple strategies, encourages a tolerance for error, and builds an appreciation of the power of inexact values in making decisions. The development of estimation skills helps dispel the one-right-answer syndrome often associated with exact computation. Research has also shown that students are often reluctant to estimate because they are more comfortable with exact answers. Thus they are unaware of how powerful estimation can be, both in and out of school.

The activities in this section will help students develop an appreciation for estimation and will challenge them to think about what numbers to use and how to use them.

Make an Estimate

Number Sense Focus

- Estimation

Number Focus

- Activities 1–3: Whole numbers

Mathematical Background

The majority of calculations that adults perform every day are estimates, for which there is seldom a "right" answer. Students must develop the ability and confidence to use what they know to make their best estimates given the circumstances and to make sensible decisions about the necessary degree of accuracy. An important part of such awareness is the development of personal referents, or *benchmarks,* which can form the basis for making good estimates.

Using the Activities

In these activities, students make estimates in a variety of situations.

1. Show the first part of Activity 1 to the students. If a two-story building is visible, make it the focus of the challenge. Invite students to work in pairs to make their estimates and to prepare explanations of their estimation strategies.

2. Invite students to share solutions and strategies for each measurement. For example:

   - "I think I would fit five times up the side of a two-story building. I'm less than 2 meters tall, so it must be less than 10 meters high; maybe about 8 meters."

   - "I think each ceiling tile is about 1 square yard, and I estimate about 100 tiles, so the area of the ceiling is about 100 square yards."

3. Activity 2 uses a standard brick as an object of comparison for all the estimates. You may want to show students a brick and discuss its size—for example, a brick about $2\frac{1}{2} \times 3\frac{3}{4} \times 8\frac{1}{4}$ inches ($58 \times 95 \times 210$ millimeters) weighs about six pounds (less than 3 kilograms). As students work, reassure them that they will not always know all the facts necessary to make a very close estimate. They must decide on the factors that are relevant and then make their best estimate. Encourage them to explain their thinking as they present their estimates. Discuss the range of estimates and the assumptions on which they were based.

4. For the estimates in Activity 3, students must make some assumptions (factors that influence the outcome); their estimates will reflect those assumptions. For example, in part 2, students will need to estimate the average weight of a spectator; you may want to bring up the idea that it is likely that some heavy people and some children will be at the game. Again, emphasize the importance of the estimation strategies rather than the exactness of the estimates.

Extending the Activities

- Have students write accounts of how they made their estimates, especially for those in Activity 3.

- Ask students to write their own estimation questions and share and discuss them in groups.

Make an Estimate

Make the best estimate you can for each measure.
Explain how you made your estimates.

1. The height of a two-story building

2. The capacity of a wheelbarrow

3. The volume of a brick

4. The weight of a bookcase

5. The area of the classroom ceiling

6. The length of a car

7. The length of the chalkboard

8. The weight of an adult

9. The perimeter of a basketball court

10. The area of a piece of notebook paper

Make an Estimate

In your mind, picture a typical brick. Now, estimate an answer for each question, and explain how you made your estimate.

1. How many bricks would fit across the classroom?

2. How many bricks would fit in an ordinary suitcase? How much would the suitcase weigh?

3. How many bricks would weigh the same as you?

4. How many bricks would it take to cover the top of your desk?

5. How many layers of bricks would reach your height?

6. If you put a brick in a bucket of water, about how much would the water level rise?

7. How many bricks would reach 100 yards?

8. Estimate the height of a stack of 100 bricks. 1000 bricks.

Make an Estimate

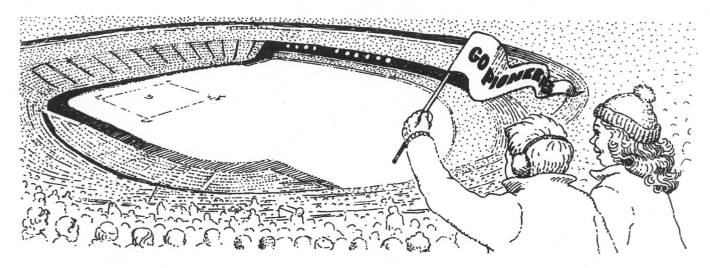

1. If 100,000 spectators are at a ball game, about how long would it take for them to all leave the stadium?

2. About what would be the combined weight of these 100,000 spectators?

3. If each spectator were carrying the amount of money equal to what the average student in the class has now, about how much money would the 100,000 spectators have altogether? Compare your estimate with others in your class. What makes your estimates different?

4. If 100,000 spectators stood in a single line, about how long would the line be?

5. If the line of spectators walked at about 5 miles per hour, how long would a single-file parade of the 100,000 people take to pass?

EXPERIENCE 9
∙∙∙∙∙∙∙∙∙∙∙∙∙∙∙∙∙∙∙∙∙∙∙∙∙∙∙

Estimating with Benchmarks

Number Sense Focus

- Estimation
- Mental computation

Number Focus

- Activities 1–3: Whole numbers

Mathematical Background
∙∙∙∙∙∙∙∙∙∙∙∙∙∙∙∙∙∙∙∙∙∙∙∙∙∙

Benchmarks are helpful for making estimates. For example, your height and weight are useful benchmarks for estimating someone else's height and weight. Estimations often involve ratios: "The shadow of that tree is at least three times the length of my shadow. I am over 5 feet tall, so that tree must be over 15 feet tall." This conclusion shows numbers being used in a thoughtful and meaningful way.

Using the Activities
∙∙∙∙∙∙∙∙∙∙∙∙∙∙∙∙∙∙∙∙∙∙∙∙∙∙

1. As a warm-up, ask students to estimate the height of the school or a particular tree or building, and to describe how they made their estimate. For example:

   - "The school is about 30 feet high. Each floor is about 10 feet high, and it has 3 floors."

   - "The school is about 35 feet high. Each floor is about 10 feet high, and there is space between floors and also a roof."

   As you discuss their strategies, highlight benchmarks that they used in making their estimates.

2. Before showing Activity 1, ask: Is the Statue of Liberty more or less than 500 feet tall? Let them share their ideas and explanations. If no rationale other than guesses exists, show the transparency. Ask: Is the

Statue of Liberty more than 300 feet tall? How do you know? How does the Gateway Arch serve as a benchmark?

3. As students estimate the heights of the other structures, keep them focused on the approximate heights that can be estimated from the visual information.

4. Before showing Activity 2, ask the class to estimate the distance in miles from San Diego to New York City if you were to fly in a straight line. Discuss the various answers and how students made their estimates. Show the map, and have the class estimate the other distances. Point out the distance from St. Louis to New York City, and encourage students to use it as a benchmark.

5. Follow a similar procedure for Activity 3.

Solutions

Activity 1

Accept any reasonable answers. Approximate measures in feet: Sears Tower 1454, Eiffel Tower 984, Statue of Liberty 305, Sphinx 240, Washington Monument 555.

Activity 2

Approximate air-distance mileage is reported here, but accept any reasonable answers.

1. 1003   2. 2435   3. 1637   4. 790   5. 2503

Activity 3

1. Venus
2. Mercury, Mars
3. 10 to 12 times
4. half
5. Neptune

Extending the Activities

• •

- Ask students to choose a benchmark and make an estimate of an object using that benchmark. Have them ask another student to use the same benchmark to estimate the object, and then compare answers.

- Ask students to research how measurements of planets are estimated.

Estimating with Benchmarks

The Gateway Arch is 630 ft high.

About how tall is each of the other structures?

Estimating with Benchmarks

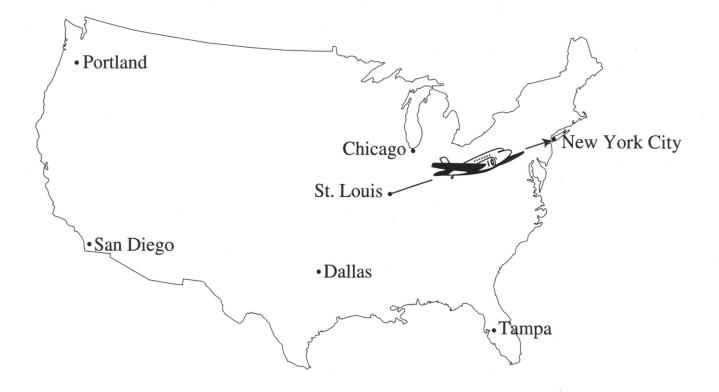

The air distance from St. Louis to New York City is 832 miles. Estimate the distance between

1. New York City and Tampa

2. New York City and San Diego

3. Dallas and Portland

4. Chicago and Dallas

5. Portland and Tampa

Estimating with Benchmarks

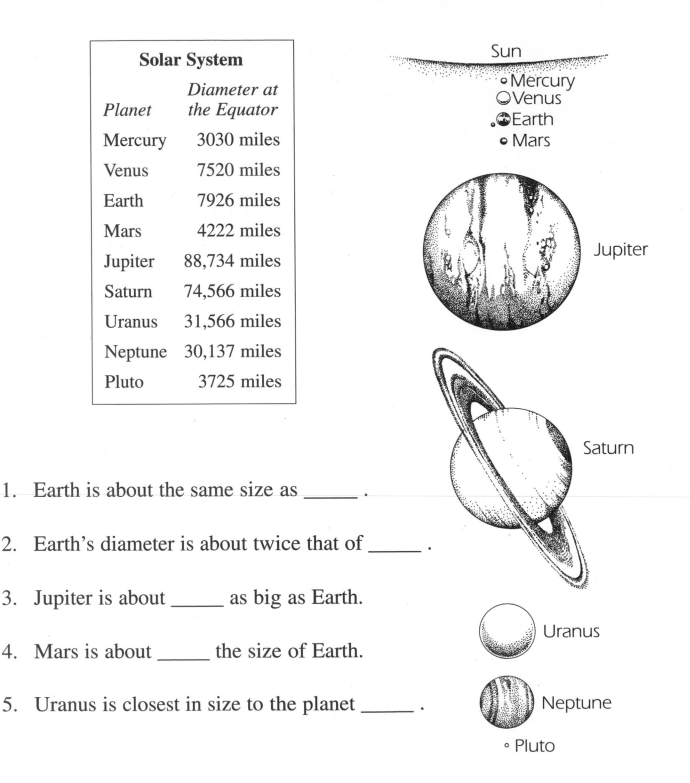

Solar System	
Planet	*Diameter at the Equator*
Mercury	3030 miles
Venus	7520 miles
Earth	7926 miles
Mars	4222 miles
Jupiter	88,734 miles
Saturn	74,566 miles
Uranus	31,566 miles
Neptune	30,137 miles
Pluto	3725 miles

Sun
Mercury
Venus
Earth
Mars

Jupiter

Saturn

Uranus

Neptune

Pluto

1. Earth is about the same size as _____ .

2. Earth's diameter is about twice that of _____ .

3. Jupiter is about _____ as big as Earth.

4. Mars is about _____ the size of Earth.

5. Uranus is closest in size to the planet _____ .

Under or Over?

Number Sense Focus

- Estimation
- Number relationships

Number Focus

- Activity 1: Fractions
- Activity 2: Decimals
- Activity 3: Fractions and decimals

Mathematical Background
. . . .

Recognizing when fraction or decimal values are near the familiar benchmarks of zero, one half, and one helps us produce quick estimates for judging the reasonableness of results or deciding whether an answer will be over or under a particular value. For example, recognizing that $\frac{4}{9}$ and $\frac{5}{12}$ are each less than $\frac{1}{2}$ allows us to quickly and confidently estimate that their sum is less than 1. It also suggests that the result will be close to 1, so the answer $\frac{9}{21}$ is obviously not reasonable.

Using the Activities
. . . .

1. As a warm-up, write $\frac{\bigcirc}{\square}$ on the board. Ask students for numbers to fill in the $\bigcirc$ and $\square$ to make fractions less than $\frac{1}{2}$. Make a list of their suggestions; for example, $\frac{3}{8}$, $\frac{4}{11}$, $\frac{5}{11}$, $\frac{4}{12}$, $\frac{5}{12}$, and $\frac{44}{91}$. Discuss any patterns the students observe in the list. For example, the denominator is always more than twice the numerator.

2. In Activity 1, ask students to explain how they used estimation and benchmarks to answer each question. If you explore these as a class, you might focus on a particular question, then ask students to make an estimate and decide. Ask them to show thumbs up or down. Thumbs up means it is over the given estimate; thumbs down means it is under the given estimate.

3. As a warm-up for Activity 2, you might make a list of decimals less than $\frac{1}{2}$, or near 1, or near but greater than $\frac{1}{2}$, and discuss the patterns students see.

4. Activity 3 combines fractions and decimals, which will help remind students of how fractions and decimals are related.

Solutions

Activity 1

1. Yes, because one fractional part is $\frac{1}{2}$ and the other two fractional parts total more than $\frac{1}{2}$ so that plus 9 pounds is more than 10 pounds.
2. under 2
3. over 2
4. under 3
5. under 1
6. under 4
7. over 11

Activity 2

1. Answers will vary.
2. over 1
3. under 3
4. under 2
5. under 3
6. under 1
7. under 6

Activity 3

1. Possible answer: $0.89 + 1\frac{1}{12} + \frac{9}{10}$
2. under 12
3. over 16
4. over 9
5. under 3

Extending the Activities

• Ask students to write several decimals between 0.48 and 0.49.

• Ask students to write several fractions between $\frac{4}{9}$ and $\frac{5}{9}$.

• Have students make up a computation problem with at least six addends—none can be zero—and a result of between 4 and 5. Ask them to explain how they constructed their problem.

Under or Over?

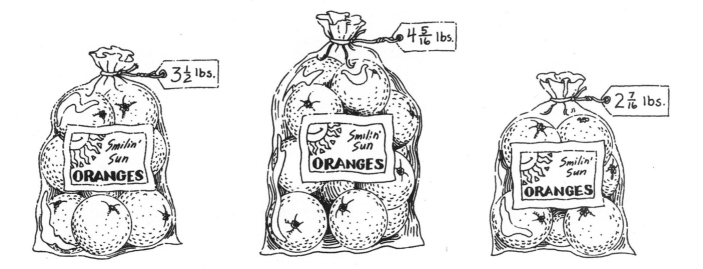

1. Does the weight of all the oranges exceed 10 pounds?
   Explain your answer.

For each sum, decide which is the better estimate, and explain your decision.

2. $\dfrac{7}{15} + \dfrac{5}{12} + \dfrac{9}{20}$

   over 2   under 2

3. $\dfrac{2}{3} + \dfrac{3}{5} + \dfrac{5}{9} + \dfrac{7}{12}$

   over 2   under 2

4. $\dfrac{41}{80} + \dfrac{1}{2} + \dfrac{19}{20} + \dfrac{4}{9}$

   over 3   under 3

5. $\dfrac{1}{9} + \dfrac{1}{10} + \dfrac{1}{12} + \dfrac{1}{20}$

   over 1   under 1

6. $\dfrac{3}{7} + \dfrac{5}{9} + \dfrac{2}{3} + \dfrac{7}{8} + \dfrac{5}{12}$

   over 4   under 4

7. $4\dfrac{3}{5} + 5\dfrac{2}{3} + 1\dfrac{7}{12}$

   over 11   under 11

Under or Over?

1. Suppose you had enough money for about 3 kilograms worth of pumpkins. Which pumpkins would you choose? Why?

For each sum, decide which is the better estimate.
Explain your decision.

2. 0.558 + 0.51498

   over 1   under 1

3. 0.5263 + 0.614 + 0.9547

   over 3   under 3

4. 0.48 + 0.5 + 0.48893 + 0.498

   over 2   under 2

5. 0.98 + 0.876 + 0.987

   over 3   under 3

6. 0.49147543 + 0.47652489

   over 1   under 1

7. 1.47 + 2.4891 + 1.89567

   over 6   under 6

Under or Over?

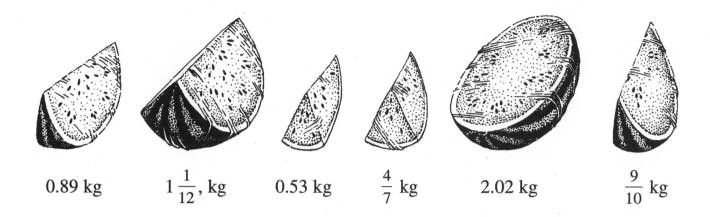

0.89 kg $1\frac{1}{12}$, kg   0.53 kg $\frac{4}{7}$ kg   2.02 kg $\frac{9}{10}$ kg

1. Which three slices of watermelon have a total mass of about
    3 kilograms?

For each sum, decide which is the better estimate.
Explain your decision.

2. $4\frac{7}{8} + 5.87 + 0.97$

    over 12   under 12

3. $7.024 + 1\frac{1}{9} + 4\frac{5}{12} + 2.495 + 1.5$

    over 16   under 16

4. $3.016 + 4.5095 + 1\frac{4}{7} + \frac{1}{20}$

    over 9   under 9

5. $0.897 + \frac{9}{10} + 0.895 + \frac{1}{30} + \frac{3}{85} + \frac{2}{25}$

    over 3   under 3

EXPERIENCE 11

•••••••••••••••••••••••••••

Estimating with Percents

Number Sense Focus

- Estimation
- Mental computation
- Multiple representation

Number Focus

- Activities 1–2: Percents

Mathematical Background

•••••••••••••••••••••••••••••••

Data are frequently presented in the form of percents. Interpreting such data often requires conversions to percents that are easier to work with mentally. For example, knowing that 58% is more than half, almost 60%, or nearly $\frac{2}{3}$ can be useful. Which of these nearly equivalent representations we choose depends on how the numbers will be used. If we estimate the African-American population of the United States as 16%, it may be sufficient to think of it as less than 20% or less than $\frac{1}{5}$. Thus, we could estimate that out of 60 million children, less than 12 million are African American. Or, it might be useful to think of 16% as about $\frac{1}{6}$, and $\frac{1}{6}$ of 60 million is 10 million. Such flexibility is critical to good number sense.

Using the Activities

•••••••••••••••••••••••••••••••

1. As a warm-up, explain that about 8%, or $\frac{1}{12}$, of people in the world are left-handed. Ask: About how many people in our class would we expect to be left-handed? Encourage students to think of appropriate compatible numbers—such as $\frac{1}{12}$ of 24, $\frac{1}{10}$ of 20, or $\frac{1}{12}$ of 36—to help make this estimate. Poll students to see how close the estimate comes to the actual number of left-handers in the class.

2. In Activity 1, show the population headline and the blood-type data. As students answer the questions, encourage estimation with compatible numbers. When students make up their own questions, ask them to include some on estimating the number of students with specific blood types in the class. (The blood type data is based on Red Cross data available in 1995. Changes in the population could change these numbers by 2010.)

3. Follow a similar procedure for Activity 2.

Solutions

Activity 1

1. 6 or 7 million
2. O
3. AB
4. O and AB *or* A and B
5. B as AB *or* A as B

Activity 2

1. Native American
2. 35 million
3. 30% to 35% or about $\frac{1}{3}$
4. Asian
5. 3% or 1.5 to 2 million

Extending the Activities

• •

- Ask students to choose a trait—such as eye color or height—and find the estimated percent of a population having certain characteristics of the trait. They can use these percentages to estimate the number of people in class (or school) with the trait.

- Ask students to find uses of compatible numbers in newspapers or magazines.

Estimating with Percents

Blood Types in the United States	
Blood type	Percent
O	46%
A	39%
B	11%
AB	4%

Using the data above, make these estimates about people in the United States.

1. In 2010, about _____ children will have type B blood.

2. In 2010, almost 30,000,000 children will have type _____ blood.

3. In 2010, about 2,000,000 children will have type _____ blood.

4. About half the people in the U.S. have either type _____ or type _____ blood.

5. About three times as many people have blood type _____ as type _____ .

Make up some questions of your own using these data.

Estimating with Percents

Predicted Racial Mixture in 2010	
Race	*Percent*
African American	16%
Asian	6%
Caucasian	58%
Hispanic	19%
Native American	1%

Using the data above, make these estimates about children in the United States.

1. In 2010, fewer than 1,000,000 children in the U.S. will be _____ .

2. In 2010, about _____ children will be Caucasian.

3. In 2010, there will be about _____ as many Hispanic children as Caucasian children.

4. In 2010, there will be between 3 and 4 million _____ children in the U.S.

5. About _____ more children will be Hispanic than African American.

Make up some questions of your own using these data.

EXPERIENCE 12

Finding Compatible Fractions

Number Sense Focus

- Estimation
- Number relationships

Number Focus

- Activities 1–3: Fractions

Mathematical Background

Many fractions used and reported daily are inexact but are close enough to make meaningful interpretations. For example, about 70 million of the 260 million people in the United States are under 18. That means about $\frac{1}{3}$ $(\frac{70}{210})$ to $\frac{1}{4}$ $(\frac{70}{280})$ of the population is under 18. Just as compatible numbers are numbers that are easy to manipulate mentally, *compatible fractions* are fractions that are easy to work with and interpret mentally. *Near-compatible fractions*—compatible fractions that are near actual fractions—are often helpful for approximating and interpreting information.

Using the Activities

In these activities, students find and use compatible fractions, which will help them to look for relationships and to become more tolerant of inexactness.

1. In Activity 1, display the circle and the three sectors of the circle. Ask students: Is one sector larger than the others, smaller, or are they all the same size? (Each sector is a slightly different size.) Now write the fractions $\frac{29}{90}$, $\frac{30}{90}$, and $\frac{31}{90}$ on the board. Ask: Which is the largest fraction? the smallest? Students will find the fractions much easier to order than the sectors, which represent these same fractions. Next, have them estimate the total of the three sectors combined. Help students recognize that although the sectors are different sizes, each is about $\frac{1}{3}$ of the circle; they are close in

size and, depending on the circumstances, could all be represented by $\frac{1}{3}$. It is often easier to work with the approximation of $\frac{1}{3}$ than with a fraction like $\frac{29}{90}$ or $\frac{31}{90}$.

2. Reveal the rest of the transparency. Ask students for compatible fractions that are easier to interpret than the given fractions.

3. In Activities 2 and 3, ask students to answer the questions, finding compatible fractions when necessary, and to explain their decisions.

Solutions

As these are estimation tasks, accept any reasonable answers.

Activity 1

1. about $\frac{10}{20}$ or $\frac{1}{2}$

2. about $\frac{70}{210}$ or $\frac{1}{3}$

3. about $\frac{12}{18}$ or $\frac{2}{3}$

4. about $\frac{80}{240}$ or $\frac{1}{3}$

5. about $\frac{6}{36}$ or $\frac{1}{6}$

6. about $\frac{90}{270}$ or $\frac{1}{3}$

7. about $\frac{25}{100}$ or $\frac{1}{4}$

8. about $\frac{250}{500}$ or $\frac{1}{2}$

9. about $\frac{45}{90}$ or $\frac{1}{2}$

10. about $\frac{400}{1200}$ or $\frac{1}{3}$

Activity 2

1. $\frac{1}{10}$

2. $\frac{2}{3}$

3. $\frac{1}{2}$

4. Borneo

5. $\frac{1}{4}$

6. Great Britain

Activity 3

1. $\frac{1}{6}$

2. $\frac{8}{100}$ or $\frac{2}{25}$

3. $\frac{6}{100}$ or $\frac{3}{50}$

4. $\frac{2}{100}$ or $\frac{1}{50}$

5. Russian

6. $\frac{1}{2}$

Extending the Activities

• •

- Name a fraction (such as $\frac{120}{365}$) and ask students to give a real-world interpretation of it (such as the part of the year completed by the end of April). Then name a fraction near the first fraction (say $\frac{121}{365}$), and ask students to interpret it. Then, use a compatible fraction to interpret the first fraction (such as that 120 days out of 365 is about 4 out of 12 months, or $\frac{1}{3}$ of the year).

- Ask students to name a fraction for the number of school days in the school year that have been completed so far.

Finding Compatible Fractions

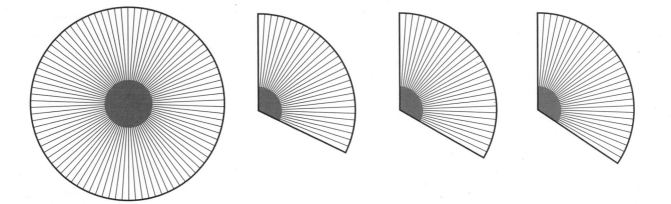

Find a close fraction to help interpret each free-throw score.

1. Travis made 9 out of 20.

2. Lance made 71 out of 220.

3. Suyuan made 11 out of 18.

4. Alex made 80 out of 239.

5. Anja made 6 out of 37.

6. Cory made 89 out of 269.

7. Jose made 24 out of 101.

8. Phalika made 243 out of 500.

9. Kevin made 44 out of 91.

10. Shondra made 411 out of 1187.

Finding Compatible Fractions

The Eight Largest Islands in the World	
Island	*Area (square miles)*
Greenland	840,000
New Guinea	306,000
Borneo	280,100
Madagascar	226,658
Baffin	195,928
Sumatra	165,000
Honshu	87,805
Great Britain	84,200

1. Great Britain is about _____ the size of Greenland.

2. Madagascar is about _____ the size of New Guinea.

3. Honshu is about _____ the size of Baffin.

4. What island is about $\frac{1}{3}$ the size of Greenland?

5. Madagascar is about _____ the size of Greenland.

6. Honshu is about the same size as _____ .

Finding Compatible Fractions

World Population ~about~ 6 BILLION people

The Eight Most Popular Languages	
Language	*Number of speakers*
Chinese	1 billion
English	470 million
Hindi	418 million
Spanish	381 million
Russian	288 million
Arabic	219 million
Japanese	126 million
German	121 million

Different versions of each language are spoken in various regions.

1. About _____ of the world speaks Chinese.

2. About _____ of the world speaks English.

3. About _____ of the world speaks Spanish.

4. About _____ of the world speaks German.

5. About $\frac{1}{20}$ of the world speaks _____

6. About what fraction of the world speaks languages other than those listed?

EXPERIENCE 13

• •

Money Matters

Number Sense Focus

- Estimation
- Relative size
- Multiple representation

Number Focus

- Activity 1: Decimals and percents
- Activity 2: Whole numbers
- Activity 3: Decimals

Mathematical Background

• •

We are familiar with our own currency and use it as a benchmark when trying to understand the ratio of one currency to another. For example, knowing that a book costs $4.35 in U.S. dollars and $6.00 in Canadian dollars provides a powerful benchmark that can be applied to other conversions. In this example, $\frac{4.35}{6}$ suggests that the Canadian dollar buys between 70% and 80% of the U.S. dollar. Since exchange rates vary daily, we generally use rough benchmarks and numerical equivalents for currency calculations. Calculators can help with exact conversions, but we must check our results for reasonableness to ensure we have used the proper conversion factor. For example, if a calculation suggests that a second book costs $12.00 in U.S. dollars and $10.00 in Canadian dollars, we must recognize that this result is inconsistent with our earlier benchmark and therefore unreasonable.

Using the Activities

• •

In these activities, focus on the buying power of each currency. Which buys the most? the least? Once an order is established, this provides a means of making estimates and producing reasonable answers.

1. As a warm-up, ask students how many nickels are in a dime. The relationship between a nickel and dime can be thought of in several ways. Two nickels are equivalent to one dime (a ratio of 2:1); one nickel is equivalent to one half of a dime (a ratio of 1:2, or 0.5). Once such a

benchmark is established, it can be used to evaluate other trades. It also provides a direct connection to exploring relationships among various currencies. Encourage students to make rough conversions mentally and then, if necessary, use calculators for more precise results.

2. Ask students if they have seen items with a price for both U.S. and Canadian currencies. Encourage sharing of experiences using currency in the two countries. Explore the questions in Activity 1, focusing on the buying power of each currency. Explain that the relative value of currencies, shown here by numbers of eggs, changes daily.

3. Follow a similar procedure for Activity 2.

4. In Activity 3, encourage students to share and explain the relationships they have included on their lists.

Solutions

Activity 1

1. It is sold in three countries—the United States, Canada, and the United Kingdom. The book costs about the same in each country. The different prices reflect the relative buying power of the currencies.
2. the British pound
3. The British pound, because it takes fewest of them to buy the book.
4. about 80%
5. about 160%

Activity 2

1. most: U.S.; least: Australian
2. More in both cases, because one U.S. dollar is worth more than one Australian or Canadian dollar.
3. Fewer, because one Canadian dollar is worth less than one U.S. dollar. More, because one Canadian dollar is worth more than one Australian dollar.
4. More than $22 in both Canadian and Australian money.
5. About 10 with a U.S. dollar; about 9 with a Canadian dollar.

Activity 3

Here are some possibilities:

The Argentine peso has the same value as a U.S. dollar. One Tanzanian shilling is worth about 100 Guatemalan quetzals. The Ukrainian karbovanet is worth less than any other currency listed.

Extending the Activities

• •

- Ask students to find items marked with prices for both Canada and the United States and to compare the exchange rates that are used.

- Ask students to find the fee a local bank charges for converting $100 of U.S. currency into, for example, Canadian or French money. Help them calculate how much money they really end up with after the conversion.

Money Matters

Current
Currencies

$14.95 US
$18.89 CAN
£9.25 UK

1. Why does this book have three prices? Are the prices really different?

2. What does the £ represent?

3. Which unit is worth the most? How do you know?

4. About what percent of the U.S. dollar was the Canadian dollar when this book was printed?

5. About what percent of the U.S. dollar was the English pound when this book was printed?

Money Matters

1. Each of these are dollars. Which of these dollars will buy the most? the least?

2. If you took $5 in U.S. money to the bank and converted it to Canadian dollars, would you receive more than or fewer than 5 Canadian dollars? Why? How about Australian dollars? Why?

3. If you exchanged $10 in Canadian money to U.S. dollars, would you receive more than or fewer than 10 U.S. dollars? Why? How about Australian dollars? Why?

4. A book has a price of $22 in U.S. currency. Would it cost more or less than $22 in Canadian money? How about in Australian money? Why?

5. You can buy 8 sacks of nuts with $1 Australian. About how many sacks of nuts can you buy with a U.S. dollar? with a Canadian dollar?

Money Matters

World Value of the Dollar

This table gives the exchange rate of the U.S. dollar against various currencies.

Argentina	(peso)	1.00
Bangladesh	(taka)	41.60
Germany	(mark)	1.524
Guatemala	(quetzal)	5.965
Iceland	(krona)	64.45
Japan	(yen)	97.63
Mali	(CFA Franc)	484.97
Malta	(lira)	2.853
Mongolia	(tugrik)	460.18
South Africa	(rand)	3.649
Tanzania	(shilling)	592.00
Ukraine	(karbovanet)	179,100.00

It takes about two Maltese lire to make one Guatemalan quetzal.

Make a list of some of the things this table tells you about these currencies.

EXPERIENCE 14

• •

People Space

Number Sense Focus

- Estimation
- Number relationships

Number Focus

- Activities 1–3: Whole numbers, fractions

Mathematical Background

• •

Population density is an interesting topic and provides opportunities for rich mathematical thinking. To compare population densities, for example, a common base must be established—and compatible numbers are powerful tools for approximating ratios and establishing a common base.

Using the Activities

• •

These activities provide opportunities to find and use compatible numbers in estimating ratios.

1. As a warm-up, have the class consider this: Colorado and Connecticut have similar populations: Colorado has about 3,566,000 people and Connecticut about 3,277,000. Do these states also have a similar *population density* (people per unit of area)? To find out, we need to know their land area. Colorado has a land area of 103,729 square miles, and Connecticut has a land area of 4845 square miles. How would you estimate their population densities? Ask students to offer some pairs of compatible numbers that could be used. You might make a list of their suggestions:

   Colorado 3,600,000 ÷ 100,000 or about 36 people per square mile
        3,500,000 ÷ 100,000 or about 35 people per square mile

   Connecticut 3,300,000 ÷ 5000 or about 660 people per square mile
        3,000,000 ÷ 5000 or about 600 people per square mile

The density we calculate depends on the compatible numbers we choose, but any of these pairs provide a reasonable estimate and show that Connecticut's population density is far greater than Colorado's. Encourage students to be flexible in choosing compatible pairs of numbers.

2. In Activity 1, ask students to make estimates of the population density of each country. Encourage them to find at least two different pairs of compatible numbers for each country and to compare the estimates each produces. Then, have them answer the questions.

3. Follow a similar procedure for Activities 2 and 3.

Solutions

Answers will vary depending on compatible numbers chosen. Accept any reasonable answer.

Activity 1

1. 700 and 540 per square mile.
2. Guatemala (12,000 ÷ 40 is about 300 people per square mile) and El Salvador (5600 ÷ 8 is about 700 people per square mile)
3. Belize (200 ÷ 10 is about 20 people per square mile) and Nicaragua (4000 ÷ 50 is about 80 people per square mile)
4. Answers will vary.
5. El Salvador, Guatemala, Costa Rica, Honduras, Panama, Nicaragua, Belize

Activity 2

1. Rhode Island (10,000 ÷ 25 is about 400 people per square km) and Connecticut (3300 ÷ 15 is about 220 people per square km)
2. Maine (1200 ÷ 80 is about 15 people per square km) and Vermont (575 ÷ 25 is about 23 people per square km)
3. Answers will vary.
4. Possible answer: Maine (1,300,000 ÷ 100,000 is about 13 people per square km); Division results by just shifting the decimal point.

Activity 3

1. South Africa (44,000 ÷ 440 = 100 people per square mile compared to 10,500 ÷ 150 = 70 per square mile)
2. Namibia (15 ÷ 3 is about 5) and Botswana (14 ÷ 2 is about 7)
3. Swaziland (910 ÷ 7 is about 130) and Lesotho (1980 ÷ 11 is about 180)
4. Answers will vary.
5. Lesotho, Swaziland, South Africa, Zimbabwe, Mozambique, Botswana, Namibia

Extending the Activities

• •

- Have students find the population and area of their state and county and use the information to estimate the state's and the county's population density.

- Challenge students to find a country with a population density greater than 1000 people per square mile.

- Ask students: If there are about 1000 people per square mile, about how many people is this per square yard?

People Space

Population of Central America

Country	Population	Area (miles²)
Belize	209,000	8867
Costa Rica	3,342,000	19,730
El Salvador	5,753,000	8124
Guatemala	10,721,000	42,042
Honduras	5,315,000	43,277
Nicaragua	4,097,000	50,880
Panama	2,630,000	29,157

1. To find the population density of El Salvador, Bill estimated $5600 \div 8$ and Angi estimated $5400 \div 10$. State the estimates from these compatible pairs. Which pair would you use? Why?

2. Which two Central American countries have the greatest population per square mile? What numbers did you use to make your estimates?

3. Which two countries have the smallest population density? What numbers did you use to make your estimates?

4. Which country was the easiest for you to generate compatible numbers to estimate population density?

5. Arrange the countries in order of population density.

People Space

Population of New England		
State	*Population*	*Area (km²)*
Connecticut	3,277,000	12,549
Maine	1,239,000	79,940
Massachusetts	6,012,000	20,300
New Hampshire	1,125,000	23,230
Rhode Island	1,000,000	2707
Vermont	563,000	24,887

1. Which two New England states have the greatest population per square kilometer? What numbers did you use to make your estimates?

2. Which two states have the smallest population density? What numbers did you use to make your estimates?

3. Which state was the easiest for you to generate compatible numbers to estimate population density?

4. Did you use a power of 10 for the area of any state? Why is a power of 10 easy to use as a divisor?

People Space

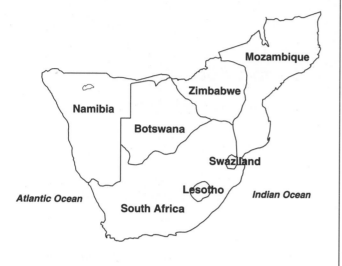

Population of Southern Africa		
Country	*Population*	*Area (miles²)*
Botswana	1,359,000	224,607
Lesotho	1,944,000	11,716
Mozambique	17,346,000	313,661
Namibia	1,596,000	318,146
South Africa	43,931,000	473,290
Swaziland	936,000	6704
Zimbabwe	10,975,000	150,872

1. Which has the greater population density, Zimbabwe or South Africa? How did you decide?

2. Which countries have a density of less than 10 people per square mile? Tell how you decided.

3. Which countries have a density greater than 100 people per square mile? Tell how you decided.

4. For which countries did you find it easiest to estimate population density? Why?

5. Arrange the countries in order of population density.

EXPERIENCE 15

Which Is Which?

Number Sense Focus

- Estimation
- Relative size

Number Focus

- Activities 1–3: Whole numbers

Mathematical Background

As visual and physical benchmarks become established in our minds, we use them to make estimations naturally. For example, if you know your home has 1500 square feet of living space, you have something familiar by which to judge the size of other homes. The units in these activities reflect those typically used in the particular sports: soccer is an international sport and the field is usually measured in metric units; baseball is an American invention. A baseball field in the United States is typically measured in feet, whereas in Canada it is likely to be reported in metric units. Working with different measurement systems provides a natural setting for making visual connections and establishing benchmarks between units.

Using the Activities

1. As a warm-up, ask students to estimate the number of pieces of paper needed to cover their desks. This will require that the class agrees on some ground rules—such as "the pieces of paper must be the same size." As students physically or mentally produce estimates, encourage them to explain their strategies. "Now ask: About how many table tennis (Ping Pong) tables will fit on a tennis court?" It may surprise some students that the dimensions of both areas are standard. Encourage students to share their ideas for making this estimate.

2. In Activity 1, reveal the collection of playing surfaces. Make sure students understand that the different surfaces are drawn to scale. Ask

them to list the surfaces in order by area. Ask what the playing areas are. Encourage students to discuss what personal experiences (benchmarks) they used. Ask students to provide specific dimensions for figures they know. For example, the bases in an infield are 90 feet apart. Dimensions for the areas are shown below, but much can be learned by encouraging students to estimate the dimensions and discussing their strategies. You might challenge students to research these dimensions and report their findings.

3. Activity 2 provides similar comparisons of larger playing surfaces.

4. Activity 3 helps connect the concept of an acre to various playing surfaces. Which of the playing fields shown are more than an acre? Ask students to estimate the dimensions of each playing field. You might have students estimate the number of acres for larger fields, such as soccer and football fields or baseball stadiums.

Solutions

Activity 1

A. table tennis table, 9 ft × 5 ft
C. wrestling mat, 12 m × 12 m
E. basketball court, 26 m × 14 m

B. tennis court, 78 ft × 36 ft
D. baseball infield, 90 ft × 90 ft

Activity 2

A. football field, 120 yd × 53 yd
C. Olympic pool, 50 m × 21 m
E. basketball court, 26 m × 14 m

B. soccer field, 100 m × 73 m
D. ice hockey rink, 61 m × 30.5 m

Activity 3

Football and soccer fields have more area than an acre.

Baseball infield (90 ft × 90 ft) Football field (120 yd × 53 yd) Basketball court (26 m × 14 m) Soccer field (100 m × 73 m) Olympic pool (50 m × 21 m) Tennis court (78 ft × 36 ft)

Extending the Activities

• Ask questions that encourage students to explore percent. About what percent of a basketball court is a wrestling mat? How many times larger than an Olympic-size swimming pool is a football field?

• Ask students to determine whether their school basketball court or swimming pool is regulation size.

Which Is Which?

The playing areas of five different games are represented here.

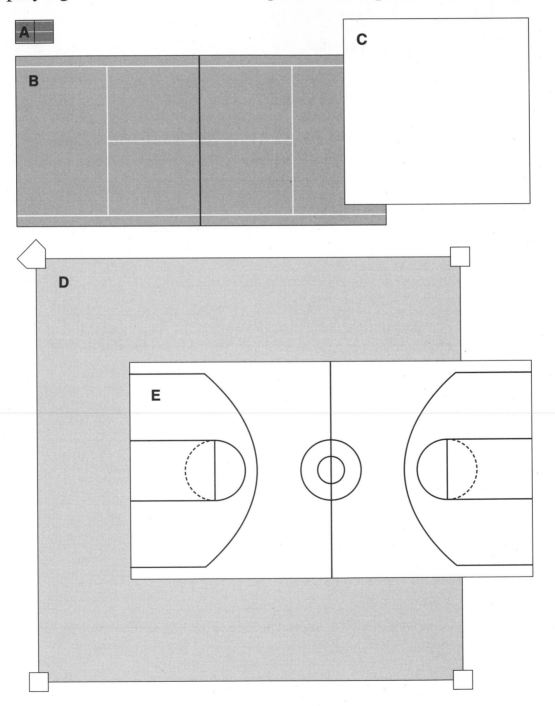

Number SENSE / Grades 6–8

Which Is Which?

These figures represent other places where different sports are played.

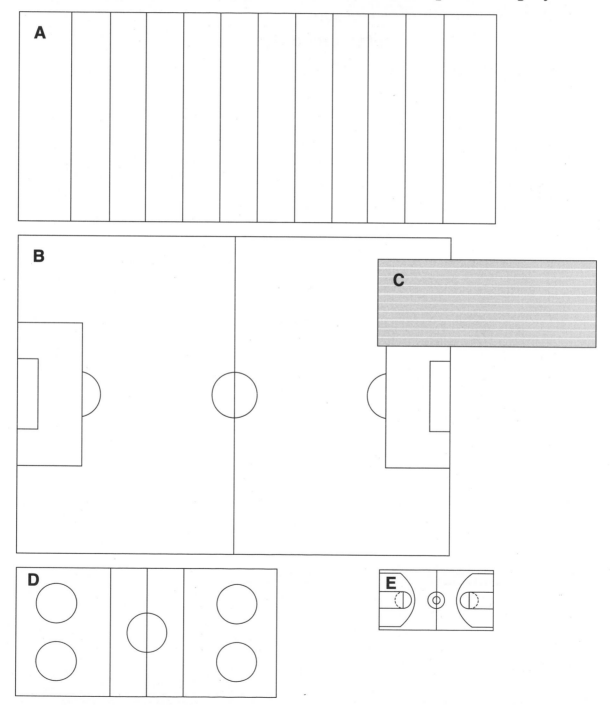

Which Is Which?

The dashed square represents one acre.
Each side is just under 209 feet long,
giving an area of about 43,560 square feet.
The other figures are sports areas.

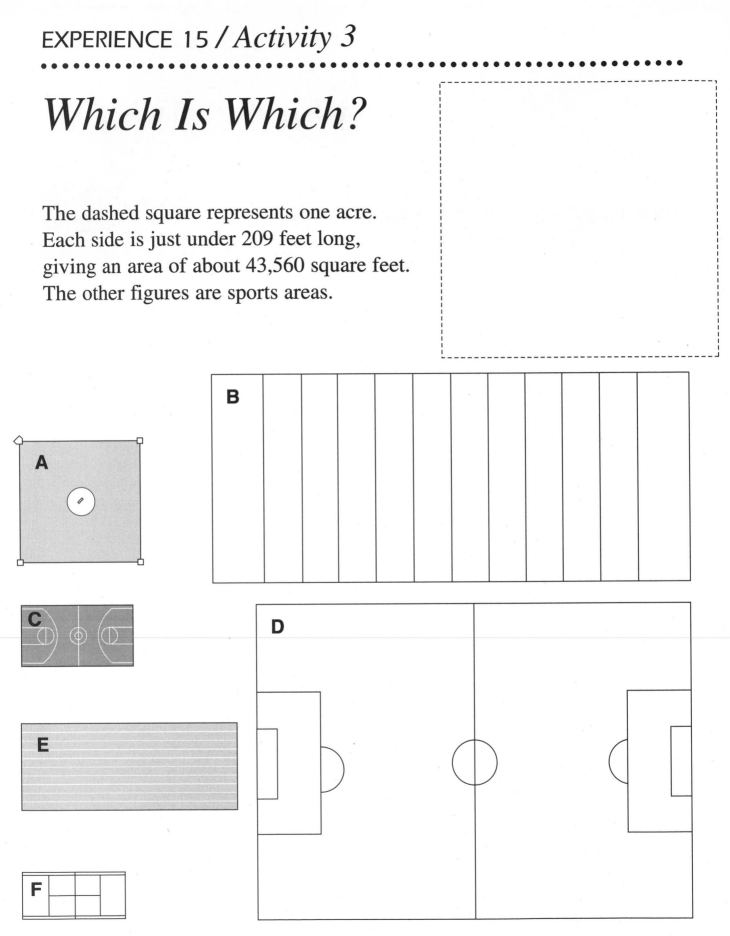

Number SENSE / Grades 6–8

Exploring Relative Size

An awareness of the relative size of numbers requires a knowledge of strategies for relating the sizes of numbers, but it also involves personal judgment and decision making. For example, is A.D. 1800 relatively recent? A scholar of ancient history would likely answer this question differently from a scholar of contemporary history. In terms of a human life span, 1980 is very recent to some people and ancient history to others. Clearly, personal knowledge, experience, and judgment are reflected in any decision about the relative size of numbers.

An understanding of the relative size of whole numbers and decimals depends on an understanding of place value. However, the relationships between whole numbers and decimals often result in confusion as students transfer experiences from one to the other. For example, place value quickly establishes that 4805 is larger than 980; yet, for decimals such as 0.9 and 0.4805, students often confuse the number of digits with their relative size. Strategies for comparing decimals include the technique of comparing them to critical benchmarks such as 0, 0.5, and 1.

Students also need practice with placing fractions in relation to other fractions. Strategies for comparing the sizes of fractions include understanding how fractions with equal numerators or denominators, such as $\frac{1}{5}$ and $\frac{1}{6}$, or $\frac{3}{7}$ and $\frac{4}{7}$, are related, and an ability to compare fractions to critical benchmarks such as 0, $\frac{1}{2}$, and 1.

A feel for the relative size of numbers is important for making estimates. Depending on the circumstances, 1000, 900, 850, and 858 could all be good estimates for 857.6, because they are all relatively near it; however, 80, 90, 8000, and 9000 are not reasonable estimates, because they are relatively much smaller or larger.

The ability to move easily among fractions, decimals, and percents in making comparisons is often important. Suppose Tisha scored 34 out of 45 on her test. Is that good? Her brother scored 70%. How does that compare with Tisha's performance? Much worse? Slightly better? About the same? A person with good number sense does not usually need to do exact comparisons to answer such questions. For example, we could reason that Tisha's score is equivalent to 68 out of 90, and her brother scored only 2 points more out of a possible 100, which is enough of an estimate to make it clear that Tisha's is a better score.

Where Are You?

Number Sense Focus

- Relative size
- Estimation

Number Focus

- Activities 1–3: Fractions

Mathematical Background

A region that is subdivided offers visual clues for the naming of fractions. Recognizing $\frac{1}{4}$, for example, is made easier by dividing a two-dimensional, regular shape into quarters or a number line into fourths. Will the same model help in naming $\frac{1}{3}$? If we know the relative sizes of $\frac{1}{3}$ and $\frac{1}{4}$, we know that $\frac{1}{3} > \frac{1}{4}$, so we know that $\frac{1}{3}$ of a shape represents more than $\frac{1}{4}$.

Using the Activities

1. As a warm-up, draw a number line and label the endpoints 0 and 4 (or some other numbers). Ask students what point is halfway between these points *(2)* and one fourth of the way between 0 and 4 *(1)*. Then, ask: Is one third of the way more than one fourth? *(yes)* Is one fifth of the way more than one fourth? *(no)*

2. In each activity, make sure students recognize the relationship between the sides of the figure and the fractional parts represented. In Activity 2, $\frac{2}{8}$ represents two complete sides of the octagon. In Activity 3, $\frac{2}{10}$ represents two complete sides of the decagon.

3. Have students work in groups to draw each polygon and to share their results as the questions are discussed. Ask additional questions that encourage them to find other positions on the polygons and to estimate fractions between the vertices.

4. In Activities 2 and 3, check where students have placed their finger on the polygon and how they have named that position.

Solutions

Activity 1

1. a. on B
   b. between B and C
   c. between A and B
   d. between C and D
   e. between C and D
2. A, X, B, W, C, Y, Z, D
3. a. 60 meters
   b. between D and A

Activity 2

1. between G and H
2. Answers will vary. Vertices represent eighths. Encourage students to focus on the relationship distance traveled + distance remaining = 1. If you have gone $\frac{1}{8}$, you have $\frac{7}{8}$ farther to go.
3. between D and E
4. between C and D
5. 240 meters; between B and C

Activity 3

1. Answers will vary. Vertices represent tenths.
2. between D and E; possible answer: 0.35, $\frac{35}{100}$
3. between I and J; possible answer: $\frac{85}{100}$, 0.85
4. between G and H; possible answer: 0.67
5. Answers will vary. Possible answer: near D; 0.3; 300 meters

Extending the Activities

• •

- Have students estimate fractions, represented as positions on regular polygons, that are near the familiar benchmark of $\frac{1}{2}$.

- Challenge students to make other regular polygons and estimate different positions around them.

- As a class, map out a hiking expedition with campsites, rest areas, and places of interest, and decide what site you would be near n of the way through the trip, where n takes on different fractional values.

Where Are You?

Start →

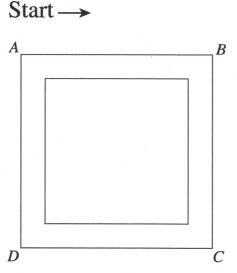

Before each question, begin at vertex *A*.

1. About where will you be when you are

    a. $\frac{1}{4}$ of the way around the square?

    b. $\frac{1}{3}$ of the way around? Mark this point *W.*

    c. $\frac{1}{5}$ of the way around? Mark this point *X.*

    d. $\frac{3}{5}$ of the way around? Mark this point *Y.*

    e. $\frac{2}{3}$ of the way around? Mark this point *Z.*

2. If you started at *A* and walked around the square, in what order would you encounter your letters?

3. Suppose the distance around the square was 100 meters.

    a. How many meters is $\frac{3}{5}$ of the way around?

    b. If you traveled about 80 meters from the start, what letters would you be between?

Where Are You?

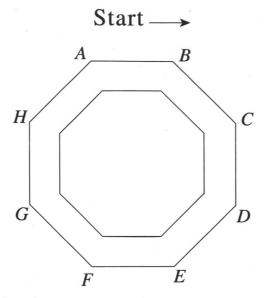

Start ⟶

Before each question, begin at vertex *A*.

1. Where will you be when you have gone $\frac{7}{8}$ of the way around the octagon?

2. Place your finger on a vertex. How far will you have gone when you have reached that vertex? How much farther do you have to go to make a complete trip?

3. Where would you be if you went almost but not quite half the distance around the octagon?

4. Where would you be if you went about $\frac{1}{3}$ of the distance around?

5. Suppose the distance around the octagon is 1200 meters. About how many meters would you have traveled if you were $\frac{1}{5}$ of the way around? Where would you be?

Where Are You?

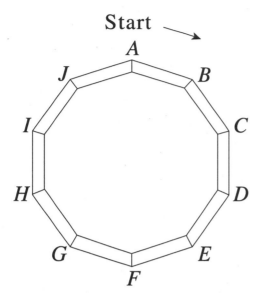

Before each question, begin at vertex *A*.

1. Place your finger on a vertex. How far will you have gone when you reach that vertex? How much farther do you have to go to make a complete trip?

2. Where will you be when you have gone between $\frac{3}{10}$ and $\frac{4}{10}$ of the distance around the decagon? Name a decimal and a fraction to describe your location.

3. Where will you be when you have gone between $\frac{8}{10}$ and $\frac{9}{10}$ of the distance around? Name a fraction and a decimal to describe your location.

4. About where would you be if you went $\frac{2}{3}$ of the distance around? Name a decimal to describe your location.

5. Suppose the distance around the decagon was 1 kilometer. About where will you be when you have gone more than $\frac{1}{4}$ but less than $\frac{1}{3}$ of the distance around? How would you write this as a decimal? About how many meters have you traveled?

EXPERIENCE 17

When Did It Happen?

Number Sense Focus

- Relative size
- Estimation

Number Focus

- Activities 1–3: Whole numbers

Mathematical Background

The end of a decade, century, and millennium is an opportunity to reflect on the occurrence of major events. Children in school today will live most of their lives in the twenty-first century, which begins in 2001. Students often measure time by their personal benchmarks, such as their grade, their birthday, and special or disturbing events. Providing opportunities for students to construct and use meaningful benchmarks helps facilitate their conceptual development of time and naturally integrates mathematics with historical and scientific topics.

Using the Activities

These activities provide a number-line model for encouraging students to think about the relative locations in time of various events.

1. As a warm-up, draw a number line on the board and label the endpoints 1980 and 2000 (or other appropriate years). Ask students to show about where they were born, began first grade, learned to ride a bicycle, and other personal benchmarks they want to share. Then, ask how they established these benchmarks. For example, if they recalled learning to ride a bike after first grade, the first-grade benchmark was used to establish the order of the events.

2. In Activity 1, ask students to locate the events on the timeline, showing how they are locating them and the benchmarks they are using. Dates are provided in the answers, but focus on the relative order of the events rather than precise dates.

3. Follow a similar procedure for Activities 2 and 3.

Solutions

Activity 1

1.	1927	4.	1914
2.	1945	9.	1917 (John Kennedy)
3.	1969	10.	1981

Activity 2

1.	1970s	6.	1920s
2.	1990s	7.	1900s
3.	1980s	8.	1910s
4.	1930s	9.	1940s
5.	1960s	10.	1950s (patented in 1960)

Activity 3

1.	1582	6.	about 570–632
2.	1337–1453	7.	2001
3.	1564–1616	8.	1929–1968
4.	1475–1564	9.	1642–1727
5.	1879–1955	10.	1833–1896

Extending the Activities

• Have students construct a timeline and locate and label five significant events of their choice along it.

• Ask students to identify five significant events in their lives and place them on a timeline.

• Have students construct a timeline into the twenty-first century, identify future personal events—such as graduation from high school or college, buying a car, or taking a major trip—and estimate about where each event should be placed.

When Did It Happen?

```
├──────────────────────────────────────────────────────┤
1900                                                  2000
```

About where should each event be placed on the timeline?

1. the first nonstop flight from New York to Paris

2. the end of World War II

3. the first space walk on the moon

4. the year the Panama Canal was opened

5. 1950

6. this year

7. the year of your birth

8. the birth of one of your parents

9. the birth of the first president born in the twentieth century

10. the first space shuttle flight

When Did It Happen?

1900 1910 1920 1930 1940 1950 1960 1970 1980 1990 1999

These items were each invented during a different decade of the twentieth century. In which decade was each invented?

1. personal computer

2. virtual reality interactive software

3. compact disk

4. parking meter

5. microwave oven (for the home)

6. television

7. electric washing machine

8. stainless steel

9. atomic bomb

10. laser

When Did It Happen?

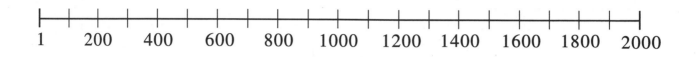

Decide about where the following events should be placed on this timeline of the first through the twentieth centuries.

1. our current calendar was established

2. The Hundred Years' War

3. Shakespeare lived

4. Michelangelo lived

5. Albert Einstein lived

6. Muhammad lived

7. start of the twenty-first century

8. Martin Luther King Jr. lived

9. Sir Isaac Newton lived

10. Alfred Nobel lived

Which Is Largest?

Number Sense Focus

- Relative size
- Number relationships
- Mental computation

Number Focus

- Activity 1: Whole numbers and fractions
- Activities 2–3: Whole numbers, decimals, and fractions

Mathematical Background

Equivalent mathematical expressions can look different, such as 10^3 and 1000 or 6! and $6 \times 5!$. Other expressions, such as 3^4 and 4^3, look similar but are not equal. Students must learn to examine such expressions carefully.

Using the Activities

These activities provide practice in interpreting similar expressions through the use of mental computation.

1. As a warm-up, show a few pairs of representations—such as 45 and 54, $\frac{3}{7}$ and $\frac{7}{3}$, or $5\frac{4}{9}$ and $\frac{54}{9}$—and ask students to describe what each pair has in common and how each pair is different.

2. Show the pairs of numbers in Activity 1. Make sure students understand that they are to find the equivalent pairs and to find the largest expression in each of the other pairs. Encourage them to look at the values and find an easy way to decide rather than to compute. Let students share their reasoning.

3. Follow a similar procedure for Activity 2. Some of the exercises in Activity 3 may require computation, but the primary purpose of these activities is to encourage students to think about the numbers rather than to compute with them.

Solutions

Given here are possible ways to reason about the problems.

Activity 1

1. $51 + 53 + 49 + 54$ because each of the four numbers is greater than 45.
2. $4 \times 3\frac{2}{5}$ because you are multiplying by something larger than 3.
3. $8 \times (2 + 3)$ because you are multiplying the 3 by 8.
4. equivalent pair
5. $15 \div \frac{2}{3}$ because division by $\frac{2}{3}$ produces a result larger than multiplication.
6. 170×50 because the other product is 0.
7. $400 \times 100 - 100$ because the other product is 0.
8. $\frac{3}{5} \div \frac{1}{2}$ because the divisor is less than the dividend.
9. equivalent pair
10. $25 \times 4 \times 85$ because $25 \times 4 > 80$.

Activity 2

1. 4 because each of the four addends is less than 1.
2. 1 because the divisor, $\frac{2}{3}$ is larger than the dividend, $\frac{1}{2}$, so the quotient is less than 1.
3. equivalent pair
4. $\frac{1}{2}(80 \times 200)$ because 20 is less than 200.
5. $35 \div 0.2$ because 0.2 is less than 0.7.
6. $360 \times \frac{4}{5}$ because $\frac{4}{5}$ is greater than $\frac{3}{4}$.
7. 1.2×2.7 because 1.2 is greater than 1.18.
8. 1 because both factors are between 0 and 1 so the product is less than 1.
9. 2 because three of the four addends are less than $\frac{1}{2}$.
10. 30×1.1 because 1.1 is greater than 0.988.

Activity 3

1. 2^1 because $2 > 1$.
2. 3^2 because $9 > 8$.
3. 4^5 because $1024 > 625$.
4. 2^6 because $64 > 36$.
5. 2^0 because $1 > 0$.
6. 25% of 100 because $100 > 95$.
7. equivalent pair
8. equivalent pair
9. 15% of 80 because $12 > 6$.
10. 100% of 450 because $450 > 4.5$.

Extending the Activities

- Ask students to construct numbers that look different but represent the same value (such as 4^2 and 2^4 or 3×4^2 and $96 \div 2$).

- Ask students to construct a computation (such as 800×0.45) and write other ways to represent it (80×4.5 or 8×45).

- Ask students to arrange the following in order of size: 33, 3^3, 3×3, 3.3, $3 \times 3!$, $\frac{3}{3}$, 33!, and .33.

- Challenge students to make as many different expressions as possible using three 2s and then arrange them in order of size.

Which Is Largest?

Find which of the following pairs of numbers are equivalent. For the other pairs, tell which is greater, and explain how you know.

1. 45×4

   $51 + 53 + 49 + 54$

2. $4 \times 3\frac{2}{5}$

   $4 \times 2\frac{3}{5}$

3. $8 \times (2 + 3)$

   $8 \times 2 + 3$

4. $80 \times 20 \times 5$

   $8 \times 2 \times 500$

5. $15 \times \frac{2}{3}$

   $15 \div \frac{2}{3}$

6. $17 \times 0 \times 50$

   170×50

7. $400 \times 100 - 100$

   $400 \times (100 - 100)$

8. $\frac{1}{2} \div \frac{3}{5}$

   $\frac{3}{5} \div \frac{1}{2}$

9. $2 \times 30 + 30$

   3×30

10. $25 \times 4 \times 85$

    80×85

Which Is Largest?

Find which of the following pairs of numbers are equivalent. For the other pairs, tell which is greater, and explain how you know.

1. $\dfrac{2}{3} + \dfrac{3}{4} + \dfrac{4}{5} + \dfrac{5}{6}$

    4

2. $\dfrac{1}{2} \div \dfrac{2}{3}$

    1

3. 12.5×45

    4.5×125

4. $80 \times 20 \times 0.5$

    $\dfrac{1}{2} (80 \times 200)$

5. $35 \div 0.2$

    $35 \div 0.7$

6. $360 \times \dfrac{3}{4}$

    $360 \times \dfrac{4}{5}$

7. 1.2×2.7

    1.18×2.7

8. $\dfrac{3}{5} \times \dfrac{6}{7}$

    1

9. $\dfrac{1}{3} + \dfrac{2}{4} + \dfrac{2}{5} + \dfrac{5}{11}$

    2

10. 30×1.1

    30×0.988

Which Is Largest?

Find which of the following pairs of numbers are equivalent. For the other pairs, tell which is greater, and explain how you know.

1. 2^1
   1^2

2. 3^2
   2^3

3. 4^5
   5^4

4. 6^2
   2^6

5. 2^0
   0^2

6. 25% of 95
   25% of 100

7. 15% of 85
   0.15×85

8. 15% of 60
   60% of 15

9. 7% of 40 + 8% of 40
   15% of 80

10. 100% of 450
    0.1% of 4500

State Squares

Number Sense Focus

- Relative size
- Estimation
- Reasonableness

Number Focus

- Activity 1: Whole numbers

Mathematical Background

The feeling you have for the size of your own state is a personal benchmark that helps you think about the relative size of other states. Working with the relative sizes of the 50 states develops this aspect of number sense in a geometry and geography setting.

Using the Activity

1. Show a map of the United States. If you do not have a world or U.S. map, use the map on page 108, but remind students of Hawaii and Alaska not pictured. Ask questions that focus attention on the shape of the states. Do any states look like squares? rectangles? other polygons? Why are boundaries of most states not straight lines? *(Boundaries are often formed by natural features such as rivers, oceans, and mountain ranges, and by established longitude and latitude lines.)* If possible, show the silhouette of your state on the overhead and see if students recognize it.

2. You may want to hand out paper copies of the map or have students use other maps of the United States. Students may want to cut out a piece of paper to represent 100,000 square miles, the size of Colorado, to use as a measuring tool. Ask students to name four states with an area greater than 100,000 square miles and explain how they decided. Have them name four states with an area of less than 50,000 square miles and

explain how they decided. What proportion of the states have an area less than one half the area of Colorado? ($\frac{2}{5}$ *or 40%*) What states are about the same size as Colorado?

3. Make sure students understand the idea that the squares represent the areas of several states drawn in correct proportion to one another. As students try to identify the state each square represents, focus the discussion on the reasoning they are using.

Solutions

Activity 1

Here is list of the 50 states and their approximate total (land and water) areas in square miles:

Rhode Island, 1231	Illinois, 57,918
Delaware, 2397	Georgia, 58,977
Connecticut, 5544	Florida, 59,988
Hawaii, 6450	Missouri, 69,709
New Jersey, 8215	Oklahoma, 69,903
Massachusetts, 9241	Washington, 70,637
New Hampshire, 9283	North Dakota, 70,704
Vermont, 9615	South Dakota, 77,121
Maryland, 12,297	Nebraska, 77,359
West Virginia, 24,232	Wisconsin, 80,374
South Carolina, 31,169	Kansas, 82,282
Maine, 33,741	Idaho, 83,574
Indiana, 36,420	Utah, 84,904
Kentucky, 40,411	Minnesota, 86,943
Tennessee, 42,145	Michigan, 96,706
Virginia, 42,326	Oregon, 97,093
Ohio, 44,828	Wyoming, 97,819
Pennsylvania, 45,759	Colorado, 104,100
Mississippi, 48,286	Nevada, 110,567
Louisiana, 49,650	Arizona, 114,008
Alabama, 52,237	New Mexico, 121,598
North Carolina, 52,672	Montana, 147,048
Arkansas, 53,182	California, 158,869
New York, 53,988	Texas, 267,277
Iowa, 56,276	Alaska, 615,230

A. Rhode Island	B. Delaware	C. Connecticut	D. Hawaii
E. Montana	F. California	G. Texas	H. Alaska

Extending the Activity

- Have students draw a square to represent their state and a square to show the relative size of each of its border states.

- Ask questions about the relative sizes of particular states. About how many Rhode Islands would fit in Connecticut? How many Texases would fit in Alaska? How many of our state would fit in Alaska? About how many Alaskas would it take to cover the United States?

- Challenge students to make a square for the largest Canadian territory and compare it to a square made to the same scale for the largest U.S. state.

- Have students look up their state's area in several different resources. What might account for the different figures they find?

State Squares

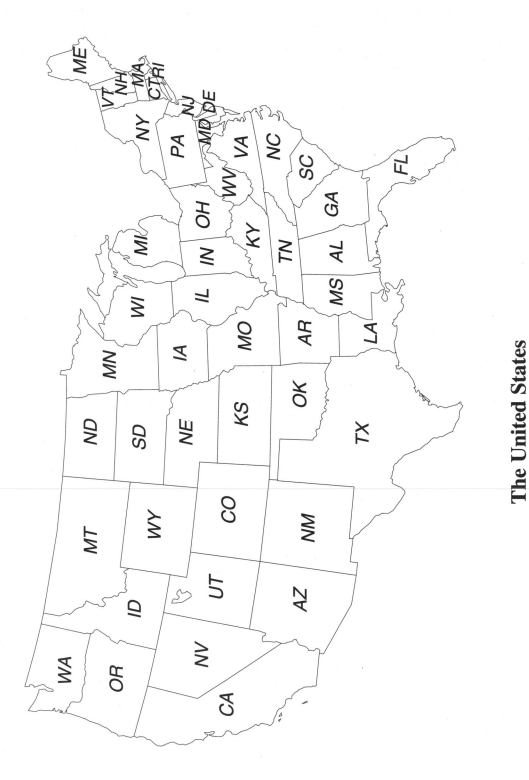

The United States

State Squares

This square represents the
area of Colorado.

Colorado

Area = 104,100 square miles

Squares A, B, C, and D represent the areas of the four smallest states.
Squares E, F, G, and H represent the areas of the four largest states. Which
state does each square represent?

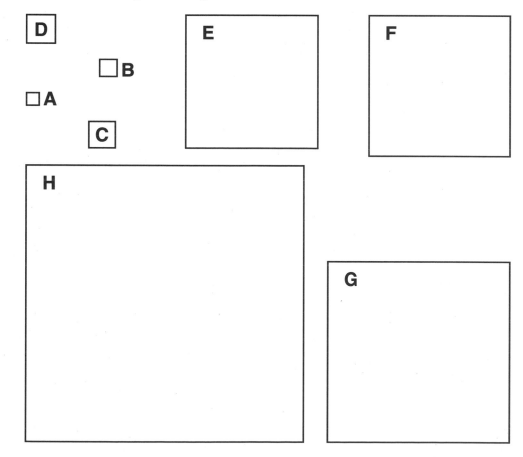

EXPERIENCE 20

About How Much?

Number Sense Focus

- Relative size
- Estimation
- Reasonableness

Number Focus

- Activities 1–2: Whole numbers, fractions

Mathematical Background

Benchmarks are handy for judging relative size. Once a benchmark is established, it can be used in different ways to solve problems. Encouraging students to use benchmarks in meaningful ways contributes to their ability to make sense of numbers.

Using the Activities

1. Show the top half of the transparency for Activity 1. Ask students to estimate the size of the piece of pizza and explain how they made their estimate.

2. Reveal that the piece is about 450 calories and ask them to estimate the number of calories in the entire pizza. Discuss how different estimates of the size of the piece affect the estimate of the number of calories in the total pizza.

3. Follow the same process on the bottom half of the transparency.

4. As you show the top of the transparency for Activity 2, Ask students which country is largest? smallest?

5. Ask students to choose one of the countries and describe the relative size of the other two countries in terms of the one they chose. A visual comparison of two countries is shown at the bottom of the transparency.

Solutions

Activity 1

Answers will vary. Focus on how students made their estimates. The piece on the top is between one fifth and one sixth of a pizza, the piece on the bottom is between one third and one half of the pizza.

Activity 2

Answers will vary depending on the countries compared. Possible answers include:

Canada is about 5 times the size of Mexico.
Australia is about 4 times the size of Mexico.
Canada is about 30 percent bigger than Australia.
Australia is a little less than two thirds the size of Canada.

Extending the Activities

• Ask students to find the population of their city to use as a benchmark. Ask them to describe the populations of other cites in relation to their city.

About How Much?

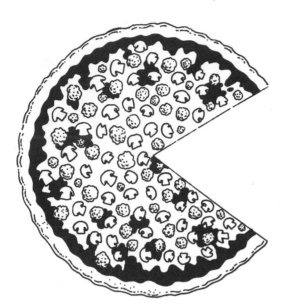

This piece of pizza has 450 calories.

About how many calories are in this pizza?

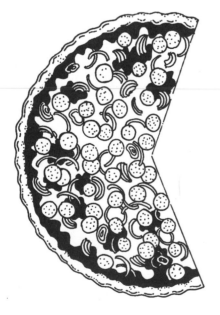

This piece of pizza has 600 calories.

About how many calories are in this pizza?

About How Much?

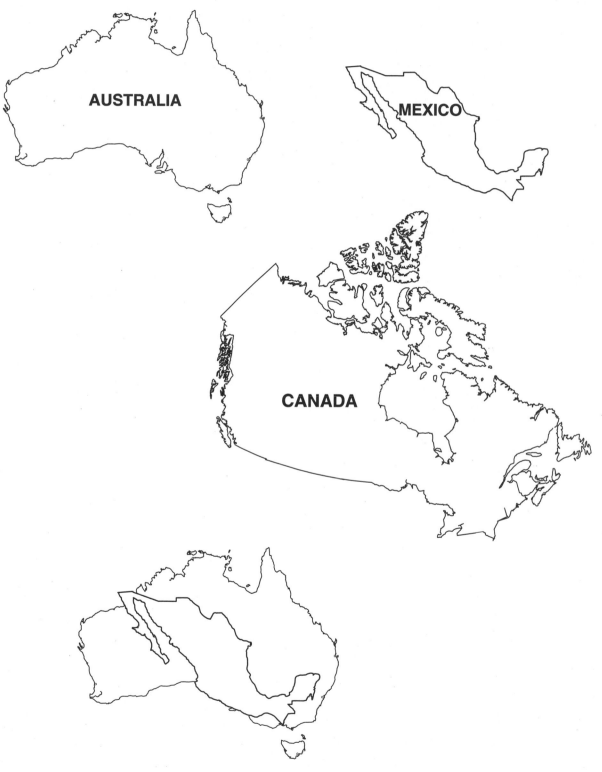

EXPERIENCE 21

• •

How Many Friday the Thirteenths?

Number Sense Focus

- Relative size
- Mental computation

Number Focus

- Activity 1: Whole numbers

Mathematical Background

• •

Calendars contain many interesting relationships and patterns.

Using the Activity

• •

1. As a warm-up, help the class determine when is the next time Friday will fall on the thirteenth. Ask: Why does this date hold special significance for some people? Make a list of their responses; for example:

   - It is the beginning of a weekend.

   - It is supposed to be lucky.

   - It is supposed to be unlucky.

   - Thirteen is unlucky, which is why many hotels don't have a floor labeled 13.

2. As a class, explore the questions in the activity. You may want to make copies of the activity to hand out to students.

Solutions

1. January 13
2. 12, 52, 3
3. Answers will vary. For January, the first day of the month must fall on Sunday; for February, Thursday. Months after February will be affected by whether the year is a leap year.

4. Yes; in a non–leap year, if February 13 is a Friday, then March 13 is also a Friday. There are 28 days in February and 28 is divisible by 7.
5. No; Halloween is always on October 31.
6. yes; September
7. 3; If Friday the thirteenth is in January of a leap year, then April and July also have Friday the thirteenths.

Extending the Activity

• •

- Is it possible to have the same number of Sundays, Mondays, Tuesdays, Wednesdays, Thursdays, Fridays, and Saturdays in a year? Why or why not?

- Have students consider this statement: The thirteenth of the month is more likely to fall on a Friday than on any other day of the week. For a discussion, check the book *Zero to Lazy Eight: The Romance of Numbers* by Alexander Humez, Nicholas Humez, and Joseph Maguire (New York: Simon and Schuster, 1993).

How Many Friday the Thirteenths?

January

Sunday	Monday	Tuesday	Wednesday	Thursday	Friday	Saturday
1	2	3	4	5	6	7
8	9	10	11	12	13	14
15	16	17	18	19	20	21
22	23	24	25	26	27	28
29	30	31				

February

Sunday	Monday	Tuesday	Wednesday	Thursday	Friday	Saturday
			1	2	3	4
5	6	7	8	9	10	11
12	13	14	15	16	17	18
19	20	21	22	23	24	25
26	27	28	29			

March

Sunday	Monday	Tuesday	Wednesday	Thursday	Friday	Saturday
				1	2	3
4	5	6	7	8	9	10
11	12	13	14	15	16	17
18	19	20	21	22	23	24
25	26	27	28	29	30	31

April

Sunday	Monday	Tuesday	Wednesday	Thursday	Friday	Saturday
1	2	3	4	5	6	7
8	9	10	11	12	13	14
15	16	17	18	19	20	21
22	23	24	25	26	27	28
29	30					

May

Sunday	Monday	Tuesday	Wednesday	Thursday	Friday	Saturday
		1	2	3	4	5
6	7	8	9	10	11	12
13	14	15	16	17	18	19
20	21	22	23	24	25	26
27	28	29	30	31		

June

Sunday	Monday	Tuesday	Wednesday	Thursday	Friday	Saturday
					1	2
3	4	5	6	7	8	9
10	11	12	13	14	15	16
17	18	19	20	21	22	23
24	25	26	27	28	29	30

July

Sunday	Monday	Tuesday	Wednesday	Thursday	Friday	Saturday
1	2	3	4	5	6	7
8	9	10	11	12	13	14
15	16	17	18	19	20	21
22	23	24	25	26	27	28
29	30	31				

August

Sunday	Monday	Tuesday	Wednesday	Thursday	Friday	Saturday
			1	2	3	4
5	6	7	8	9	10	11
12	13	14	15	16	17	18
19	20	21	22	23	24	25
26	27	28	29	30	31	

September

Sunday	Monday	Tuesday	Wednesday	Thursday	Friday	Saturday
						1
2	3	4	5	6	7	8
9	10	11	12	13	14	15
16	17	18	19	20	21	22
23	24	25	26	27	28	29
30						

October

Sunday	Monday	Tuesday	Wednesday	Thursday	Friday	Saturday
	1	2	3	4	5	6
7	8	9	10	11	12	13
14	15	16	17	18	19	20
21	22	23	24	25	26	27
28	29	30	31			

November

Sunday	Monday	Tuesday	Wednesday	Thursday	Friday	Saturday
				1	2	3
4	5	6	7	8	9	10
11	12	13	14	15	16	17
18	19	20	21	22	23	24
25	26	27	28	29	30	

December

Sunday	Monday	Tuesday	Wednesday	Thursday	Friday	Saturday
						1
2	3	4	5	6	7	8
9	10	11	12	13	14	15
16	17	18	19	20	21	22
23	24	25	26	27	28	29
30	31					

How Many Friday the Thirteenths?

1. What is the first Friday the thirteenth for the year shown in the calendar?

2. In the year shown, there are _____ thirteenths, _____ Fridays, and _____ Friday the thirteenths.

3. Choose a month. Decide on what day January 1 would need to fall for a Friday the thirteenth to occur in the month you chose. Would a leap year affect your answer? If so, how?

4. Could Friday the thirteenth ever occur in consecutive months? Explain.

5. Could Halloween ever occur on Friday the thirteenth?

6. Must every year have at least one Friday the thirteenth? If so, what is the latest month in the year that Friday the thirteenth could occur?

7. What is the greatest number of Friday the thirteenths that could occur in a year? Explain.

Exploring Multiple Representation

Numbers may be expressed in a variety of symbolic and graphical representations. For example:

- $\frac{3}{4}$ is equivalent to $\frac{6}{8}$ and 0.75 and 75%.

- 30 cents is 3 dimes or a quarter plus a nickel.

- 30 minutes is $\frac{1}{2}$ hour.

- The fraction one half may be expressed by its word name, the symbol $\frac{1}{2}$, or a drawing:

- The expression $\frac{1}{2} + \frac{1}{2} + \frac{1}{2} + \frac{1}{2}$ is the same as $4 \times \frac{1}{2}$. (Recognizing the connection between addition and multiplication can help a student better understand fraction–whole-number relationships.)

Understanding multiple representation, recognizing that some representations are more useful than others in certain problem-solving situations, and being able to generate equivalent representations are essential number sense skills.

For example, suppose a person is checking out at the market and has a bill of $8.53. The person could pay with a $10 bill and get $1.47 change. However, if the customer wanted to carry fewer coins, he or she could pay with a $10 bill and 3 pennies, and receive change of $1.50. Decomposing $8.53 into $8.50 + $0.03 provides the rationale for this option.

Activities in this section promote several ways to think about equivalent forms of numbers. Experiences in thoughtfully breaking numbers apart—decomposing—and putting them together—recomposing—in different but equivalent ways develop a useful skill. The ability to recognize and create numerical representations that simplify problems is an indication of high-level mathematical thinking.

....

Picture, Story, Symbol

Number Sense Focus

- Multiple representation

Number Focus

- Activities 1–3: Whole numbers, fractions, decimals

Mathematical Background

•••••••••••••••••••••••••••••

Mathematical knowledge can be represented with symbols, pictures or graphs, words, and real objects or actions. Mathematical understanding depends on building a network of connections among these representations.

Using the Activities

•••••••••••••••••••••••••••••

These activities provide valuable insight into the extent of students' understanding of various representations. Each problem presents information in one of three types of representation—symbols, story form, or picture or graph form—and challenges students to translate the information into the other two forms.

1. As a warm-up, write 3×2 on the board and ask students for a story and picture to accompany the expression. For example, it could generate the story, "I have three pairs of socks, so I have six socks in all," and a picture of three pairs of socks hanging on a clothesline. Explain that whichever form is given, the symbol, story, and picture must match.

2. In Activity 1, reveal one of the pictures. Ask pairs of students to work together to make a story and symbols to match the picture. Invite pairs to show their symbols and to read their story to the class.

3. Use Activities 2 and 3 in the same way. Activity 2 begins with information in story form; Activity 3 begins with information in symbolic form.

Solutions

Given below are possible answers for each part. No pictures are given. Be sure the picture matches the story. Accept any story that corresponds to the picture.

Activity 1

1. The location of the island is marked on a grid. The island is in section 5, B.
2. Each crate holds 5 rows of 3 boxes each. $5 \times 3 = 15$.
3. One store sold 100 CDs in one week, another sold about 60, and a third sold about 50. $100 + 60 + 50 = 210$.
4. Three of the 8 flowers are blue. $\frac{3}{8}$.
5. Arlene won with 11 points, Kes lost by 3 points, and Vanessa lost by 8 points. $11 > 8 > 3$.
6. On Monday I played 4 games, on Wednesday I didn't play, and on Friday I played 2 games. $4 + 0 + 2 = 6$.
7. The pie was cut into 8 pieces, and I ate 1 piece. $\frac{7}{8}$ of the pie is left.
8. Our team paired off into 4 groups of 2. $8 \div 4 = 2$.
9. Our small theater holds 100 people, and 7 chairs in the front row are always reserved, leaving 93 chairs for general seating. $100 - 7 = 93$.

Activity 2

1. $\$6 + \$9.50 = \$15.50$
2. $1.65m - 1.40m = 0.25$ m
3. $5{:}40 + 0{:}30 = 6{:}10$
4. $b - g = 4$
5. $\bigcirc \div 5 = \square$ with 2 left over
6. $\frac{2}{3}$ of 24 hours = 16 hours
7. $8 \div 4 = 2$ tasks each
8. $55 + 50 = 105$ grams
9. 150 cm $- 60$ cm $= 90$ cm

Activity 3

1. I made $36 one weekend and $54 the next, for a total of $90.
2. They deducted 25 points as a penalty from the 50 he had scored.
3. Together, the 250-gram bird and the 150-gram bird have less mass than the 450-gram bird.
4. The 1.6-yard length of material can be cut in half to make two 0.8-yard lengths.
5. They split the 70 kg of clay into two equal portions.
6. Of the two pizzas that were delivered, they only ate $\frac{3}{4}$ of one pizza.
7. He spent $765 of his $1000 poetry contest prize on a computer.
8. Alex had 1.6 pounds of cement and Su-Mei had 1.8 pounds. Together, they had 3.4 pounds.
9. The length of the side of a square with this perimeter is 3 inches.

Extending the Activities

- Challenge individuals or pairs to create several pictures, stories, or symbols to match given information.

- Have students make up sets of three different but equal representations.

Picture, Story, Symbol

Create a story and symbols to match each picture.

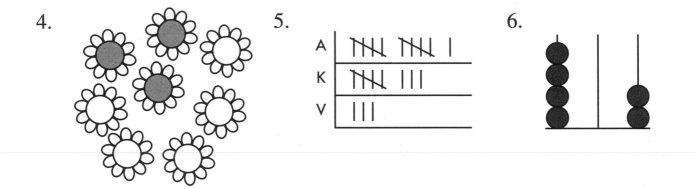

1.

2.

3.

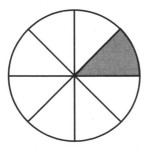

4.

5.

6.

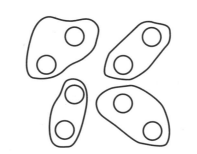

7.

8.

9.

Picture, Story, Symbol

Create a picture and symbols to match each story.

1. I bought a book for $6 and a calculator for $9.50.

2. I am 1.65 meters tall. My sister is 1.40 meters tall.

3. The program starts at 5:40 P.M. and lasts for 30 minutes.

4. There are four more boys than girls in this class.

5. Five of us shared the cookies, and there were two cookies left over.

6. Two thirds of my day is spent awake.

7. The four of us shared the eight tasks.

8. One egg weighs 55 grams, and the other weighs 50 grams.

9. I had 1.5 meters of wrapping paper. After I wrapped the gift, I had 60 centimeters left.

Picture, Story, Symbol

Create a picture and a story to match each set of symbols.

1. $36 + 54 = 90$

2. $50 - 25 = 25$

3. $250 \text{ g} + 150 \text{ g} < 450 \text{ g}$

4. $0.8 \text{ yd} + 0.8 \text{ yd} = 1.6 \text{ yd}$

5. $70 \text{ kg} \div 2 = 35 \text{ kg}$

6. $2 - \frac{3}{4} = 1\frac{1}{4}$

7. $1000 - 765 = 235$

8. $1.6 + 1.8 = 3.4$

9. perimeter $= 12$ in.

Make That Number

Number Sense Focus

- Multiple representation
- Mental computation

Number Focus

- Activity 1: Whole numbers, fractions
- Activity 2: Fractions, decimals

Mathematical Background

A given set of numbers can be combined and operated on to produce many different results. For example, $2 \times 3 \times 4 \times 5 = 120$ but $2 + 3 + 4 + 5 = 14$. Similarly, applying different operations may produce the same result; $4 + 6 + 8 + 2 = 20$ and $4 \times 6 - 8 \div 2 = 20$. Working with numbers in this way encourages students to think about numbers and the effect of operations.

Using the Activities

In these activities, students employ mental computation and their knowledge of the order of operations to produce different results from a single set of numbers.

1. As a warm-up, ask students what results they can get from forming expressions with the numbers 5 and 2. List their suggestions, and encourage a variety of responses; for example:

   $7 = 2 + 5$ $2.5 = 5 \div 2$
   $10 = 2 \times 5$ $3 = 5 - 2$
   $32 = 2^5$ $^-3 = 2 - 5$
   $25 = 5^2$ $\frac{2}{5} = 2 \div 5$.

2. Reveal the first set of numbers, or write them on the board. Give one result (880) to get things started, and ask students to use each number once and only once to create that result (for example, $20 \times 40 + 80$).

Then, ask students to find other results and list them on the board along with their name; for example:

140	Paul
$\frac{1}{160}$	Tameka
3220	Adrian
1560	Daniela

As the list grows, you might challenge students to find all the ways they can to produce one of the results listed.

3. Follow a similar procedure in Activity 2. The numeral 1 is included in both sets of numbers to remind students that 1 is both a decimal and fraction. After students complete Activity 2, ask what connections or patterns they see between the two sets of numbers. (The results should be identical, since the fraction and decimal values are the same.)

Solutions

Given here are five possibilities for each part.

Activity 1

1. $10 = 20 \times 40 \div 80$; $64{,}000 = 20 \times 40 \times 80$; $3220 = 40 \times 80 + 20$; $1640 = 20 \times 80 + 40$; $160 = 40 \times 80 \div 20$

2. $911 = 1000 - 100 + 10 + 1$; $1111 = 1 + 10 + 100 + 1000$; $2001 = 10 \times 100 + 1000 + 1$; $2 = 1000 \div 100 \div 10 + 1$; $889 = 1000 - 100 - 10 - 1$

3. $5\frac{1}{2} = 10 \div 2 + \frac{1}{2}$; $7\frac{1}{2} = 10 - 2 - \frac{1}{2}$; $16 = 10 - 2 \div \frac{1}{2}$; $24 = (10 + 2) \div \frac{1}{2}$; $19\frac{1}{2} = 10 \times 2 - \frac{1}{2}$

Activity 2

1. $1.25 = 0.5 + 1 - 0.25$; $0.25 = 1 - 0.5 - 0.25$; $0.125 = 1 \times 0.5 \times 0.25$; $2 = (1 \div 0.25) \times 0.5$; $8 = 1 \div 0.25 \div 0.5$

2. $1\frac{1}{4} = \frac{1}{2} + 1 - \frac{1}{4}$; $\frac{1}{4} = 1 - \frac{1}{2} - \frac{1}{4}$; $\frac{1}{8} = 1 \times \frac{1}{2} \times \frac{1}{4}$; $2 = (1 \div \frac{1}{4}) \times \frac{1}{2}$; $8 = 1 \div \frac{1}{4} \div \frac{1}{2}$

3. $1\frac{1}{4} = (\frac{2}{5} + \frac{3}{5}) \div \frac{4}{5}$; $1 = \frac{4}{5} - \frac{2}{5} + \frac{3}{5}$; $1.8 = \frac{4}{5} + \frac{2}{5} + \frac{3}{5}$; $\frac{6}{25} = (\frac{4}{5} - \frac{2}{5}) \times \frac{3}{5}$; $2\frac{3}{5} = \frac{4}{5} \div \frac{2}{5} + \frac{3}{5}$

Extending the Activities

- Have students choose their own sets of numbers and see how many different results they can make.

- Identify a result, and ask students to choose any three numbers and then try to use operations on the numbers to produce that result.

- Ask students to make a list of the results they can get by using the four digits in the current year. Which of these years—1976, 1999, 2000, or 2013—will produce the longest (or shortest) list of results and explain why.

Make That Number

For each set, find as many results as you can by combining the numbers.

1. ## 20   40   80

2. ## 1   10   100   1000

3. ## $\frac{1}{2}$ 10   2

Make That Number

For each set, find as many results as you can by combining the numbers.

1. **0.5**   **1**   **0.25**

2. $\dfrac{1}{2}$ **1** $\dfrac{1}{4}$

3. $\dfrac{4}{5}$ $\dfrac{3}{5}$ $\dfrac{2}{5}$

EXPERIENCE 24

• •

More Make That Number

Number Sense Focus

- Multiple representation
- Mental computation

Number Focus

- Activity 1: Whole numbers, fractions
- Activity 2: Whole numbers, fractions, decimals

Mathematical Background

• •

This experience continues the work from Experience 23. In these activities, students use three or four given numbers to produce a specified result.

Using the Activities

• •

1. Reveal the first set of numbers, or write the four numbers and the goal on the board. Make a list of how many ways students can think of to use the numbers 2, 4, 6, and 8 to make 20; for example:

    $$2 + 4 + 6 + 8 \qquad 6 \times 4 - 8 \div 2$$
    $$8 \times 4 - 2 \times 6 \qquad 8 \times 6 \div 2 - 4$$

    As students add each new solution, ask them to explain why they did what they did. For example, "First I saw that $8 \times 6 = 48$, then I used the 2 to get $48 \div 2 = 24$, and then I realized that $24 - 4 = 20$ so I knew I could write $8 \times 6 \div 2 - 4$." This is also an opportunity to discuss the order of operations and when parentheses are needed.

2. Follow a similar procedure with the other sets of numbers and with Activity 2. Challenge students to find at least three ways to produce each goal.

Solutions

Several possibilities are shown for each set of numbers.

Activity 1

1. $2 + 4 + 6 + 8$, $6 \times 4 - 8 \div 2$, $8 \times 4 - 2 \times 6$, $8 \times 6 \div 2 - 4$
2. $10 \div 2 + 5 + 0$, $10 + 5 \times 2 \times 0$, $5 \times 2 + 0 \times 10$, $10 - 0 \div 5 \div 2$
3. $10 \times 2 + 4 \times \frac{1}{2}$, $10 \div \frac{1}{2} + 4 \div 2$, $10 \times 4 \times \frac{1}{2} + 2$, $(4 + 2) \div \frac{1}{2} + 10$

Activity 2

1. $6 + 3 \div (\frac{2}{3} + \frac{1}{3})$, $6 \times 3 \div (\frac{2}{3} \div \frac{1}{3})$, $6 \div 3 \div \frac{2}{3} \div \frac{1}{3}$
2. $2 - 1 + 0 \times 0.5$, $2 \div (1 \div 0.5) + 0$, $2 \times 0.5 \times 0 + 1$, $2 \times 1 \times 0.5 + 0$
3. $2 - 4 \times 0.5 + 1$, $4 \div 1 \div 2 \times 0.5$, $4 \div 2 \times 0.5 \times 1$, $4 - 2 \div 0.5 + 1$

Extending the Activities

● ●

- Have students choose four numbers and find a goal that can be reached in several ways with their four numbers.

- Identify a goal, and ask students to choose four numbers that will produce it in at least three ways.

More Make That Number

Write as many ways as you can to make the number in the starburst by using each of the surrounding numbers once.

1.

2.

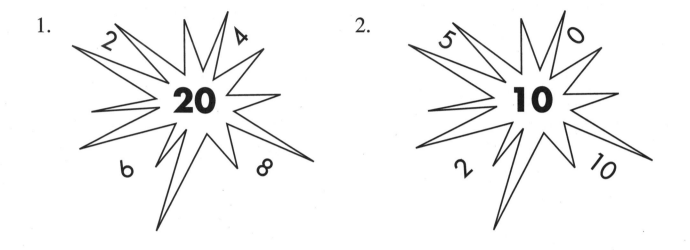

3.

More Make That Number

Write as many ways as you can to make the number in the starburst by using each of the surrounding numbers once.

1.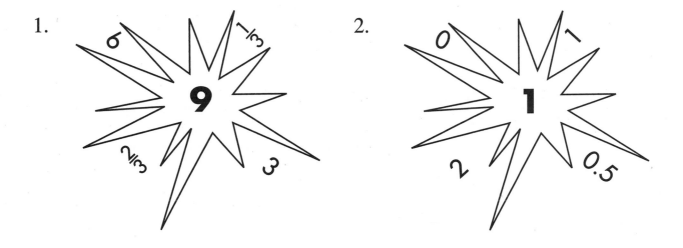

2.

3.

EXPERIENCE 25

Number This Name

Number Sense Focus

- Multiple representation
- Relative size

Number Focus

- Activities 1–4: Whole numbers

Mathematical Background

To communicate intelligently and effectively, we need to have a command of the vocabulary of numbers.

Using the Activities

In these activities, students explore number nomenclature, from the everyday to the esoteric.

1. In Activity 1, ask students to identify the number associated with each term. Help explain the meaning of terms with which they are unfamiliar.

2. In Activity 2, you may want to have dictionaries available.

3. Activity 3 gets students thinking about really large numbers. Read the large-number facts as a class.

   - There are over 260 million people in the United States.
   - If you lived a billion seconds, you would be over 30 years old.
   - The population of the earth is about 6 billion people.
   - At birth, we have about 5 trillion brain cells. At one year, we have about 100 trillion brain cells.
   - If a trillion dollars were evenly divided among every person on earth, each person would get about $200.

4. Reveal the first three rows on Activity 4. Ask students where they have heard large numbers used. Ask students what patterns they can see in the naming of large numbers. A *billion* has two groups of three zeros after 1000. A *trillion* has three groups of three zeros after 1000. Have them describe and write a large number. Reveal rows of the chart one by one. Ask them how knowing the word *centennial* might help them write a *centillion*. (*Centennial* and *centillion* have centi as a prefix, which means 100. A centillion has 100 sets of three zeros following 1000, or 10^{303}.) Students should see that once the pattern is known, very large numbers can be named.

Solutions

Activity 1

tithe, $\frac{1}{10}$; pair, couple, 2; half a dozen, 6; dozen, 12; baker's dozen, 13; score, 20; gross, 144

Activity 2

semicircle—half-circle, *semicolon*—half-colon, *semiquaver*—sixteenth note (which is half of an eighth note, called a *quaver*)
hemisphere—half a sphere, *hemistich*—half a line of poetry
decade—10 years, *decagon*—10-sided polygon, *December*—tenth month (in the Roman calendar)
nonagon—9-sided polygon, *nonagenarian*—person in his or her 90s, *novena*—9-day prayer
triangle—3-sided polygon, *triathlon*—race with 3 events, *tripod*—3-legged stand

Extending the Activities

• •

- Ask students for other connections among prefixes of mathematical words and other words, such as *bisect, bicycle,* and *bilingual.*

- Challenge students to write a sentence or story that uses large-number words in a meaningful way.

- Have students search for other real-world usage of large-number words.

- Ask if students have heard of a *googol,* a term coined by a 9-year-old. Show 10^{100} as a quicker way to write it. Ask students to estimate how long it would take to write a googol without using exponents. Then, have them time how long it actually takes.

- The word *googolplex* is 10^{googol} or $10^{10^{100}}$. How long would it take to write it without exponents?

Number This Name

Match each word to the number associated with it.

tithe

half a dozen

couple

dozen

score

baker's dozen

pair

gross

20

2

13

6

144

$\frac{1}{10}$

12

Number This Name

Find words with the same prefix, and give the meaning of each word.

semiquaver

hemisphere

semicircle

nonagon

nonagenarian

hemistitch

decagon

triathlon

decade

semicolon

novena

December

triangle

tripod

Number SENSE / Grades 6–8

Number This Name

- There are over 260 million people in the United States.

- If you lived a billion seconds, you would be over 30 years old.

- The population of the earth is about 6 billion people.

- At birth, we have about 5 trillion brain cells. At one year, we have about 100 trillion brain cells.

- If a trillion dollars were evenly divided among every person on earth, each person would get about $200.

Number This Name

Name	Power of Ten	Written
million	10^6	1,000,000
billion	10^9	1,000,000,000
trillion	10^{12}	1,000,000,000,000
quadrillion	10^{15}	1,000,000,000,000,000
quintillion	10^{18}	1,000,000,000,000,000,000
sextillion	10^{21}	1,000,000,000,000,000,000,000
septillion	10^{24}	1,000,000,000,000,000,000,000,000
octillion	10^{27}	1,000,000,000,000,000,000,000,000,000
nonillion	10^{30}	1,000,000,000,000,000,000,000,000,000,000
decillion	10^{33}	1,000,000,000,000,000,000,000,000,000,000,000
undecillion	10^{36}	1,000,000,000,000,000,000,000,000,000,000,000,000
duodecillion	10^{39}	1,000,000,000,000,000,000,000,000,000,000,000,000,000
tredecillion	10^{42}	1,000,000,000,000,000,000,000,000,000,000,000,000,000,000
quattuordecillion	10^{45}	1,000,000,000,000,000,000,000,000,000,000,000,000,000,000,000
quindecillion	10^{48}	1,000,000,000,000,000,000,000,000,000,000,000,000,000,000,000,000
sexdecillion	10^{51}	1,000,000,000,000,000,000,000,000,000,000,000,000,000,000,000,000,000
septendecillion	10^{54}	1,000,000,000,000,000,000,000,000,000,000,000,000,000,000,000,000,000,000
octodecillion	10^{57}	1,000,000,000,000,000,000,000,000,000,000,000,000,000,000,000,000,000,000,000
novemdecillion	10^{60}	1,000,000,000,000,000,000,000,000,000,000,000,000,000,000,000,000,000,000,000,000
vigintillion	10^{63}	1,000,000,000,000,000,000,000,000,000,000,000,000,000,000,000,000,000,000,000,000,000

....

Thinking About Numbers

Number Sense Focus

- Multiple representation
- Mental computation

Number Focus

- Activities 1–4: Whole numbers, decimals

Mathematical Background

••••••••••••••••••••••••••••

Representing a quantity such as 100 by factoring (such as 2×50 or 50×2) or decomposing it in other ways (such as $99 + 1$ or $50 + 50$) encourages algebraic thinking. We might think of $50 \times B = 100$ as $50 \times B = 50 \times 2$ and conclude that B must equal 2.

Using the Activities

•••••••••••••••••••••••••••

1. Each activity begins with an illustration of multiple representations. Encourage students to discuss which representation is the most useful for finding the value of the variable. In Activity 1, 100 could be thought of as $5 + 95$, but the representation 50×2 is more useful for solving the equation $50 \times A = 100$. It really helps to talk about the representations and make sure students understand the mental arithmetic involved.

2. In Activity 1, show each equation and ask how the variable A might be found. Encourage students to think about the equations mentally and to record representations as they come to mind. Subtle mathematical issues are embedded in these equations. For example, $855 \times A = 855$ requires students to think of the fact that 855×1 is the same as 855. This important idea is sometimes difficult to grasp. Learn more about students' thinking by asking such questions as, What operation did you use to find the answer? Why? Did anyone do it another way?

3. Use Activities 2, 3, and 4 in the same way. Activities 3 and 4 present two different operations in the same equation. Though Activity 4 presents the information in a slightly different form, the reasoning required is the same.

Solutions

Answers are given, but the emphasis should be on the representation of the numbers used by students and their solution strategies.

Activity 1	Activity 2	Activity 3	Activity 4
1. 2	1. 5	1. 25	1. 1
2. 1	2. 70	2. 5	2. 0
3. 0	3. 4	3. 25	3. 20
4. 2	4. 50	4. 8	4. 5
5. 32	5. 25	5. 20	5. 8
6. 15	6. 200	6. 200	6. 10
7. 1	7. 25	7. 700	7. 2
8. 9	8. 0	8. 800	8. 9
9. $4.05	9. $10.00	9. $2.98	9. 3
10. $1.01	10. $1.12	10. $0.04	10. 5

Extending the Activities

• Have students make up equations, "hide" one of the values by making it a variable, and share their equations with other students.

• Present other equations, and ask students to describe physical models that might provide another way of thinking about the numbers. For example, in part 9 of Activity 1, a 95¢ item bought for $5 will require change of $4.05.

• Invite students to make up more examples like parts 7–10 of Activity 4.

Thinking About Numbers

Think about each equation. Then, use what you know about numbers to find the value of A. Tell what representation you used.

1. $50 \times A = 100$

2. $855 \times A = 855$

3. Zero is 87 times A.

4. $8 \times A = 2 \times 2 \times 2 \times 2$

5. $A + 64 = 32 + 32 + 32$

6. $2A + 100 = 40 + 60 + 30$

7. $499 + A = 250 + 250$

8. $225 = A \times 5 \times 5$

9. $\$0.95 + A = \$5.00$

10. $\$10.00 = \$8.99 + A$

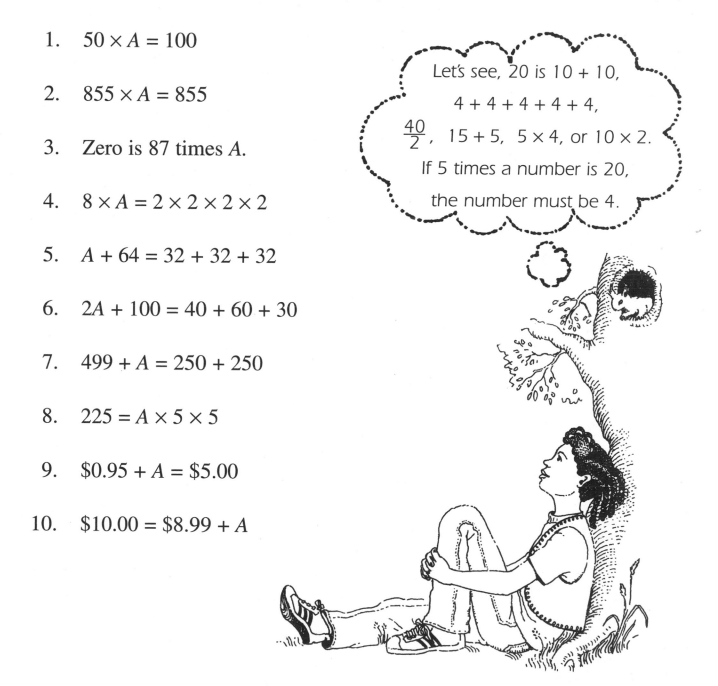

Let's see, 20 is 10 + 10, $4 + 4 + 4 + 4 + 4,$ $\frac{40}{2}$, 15 + 5, 5 × 4, or 10 × 2. If 5 times a number is 20, the number must be 4.

Thinking About Numbers

Think about each equation. Then, use what you know about numbers to find the value of *B*. Tell what representation you used.

1. $50 \times B = 250$

2. $371 = B + 301$

3. $4 \times 4 \times B = 64$

4. $75 + 25 = 50 + B$

5. $300 + 425 + 700 = 1400 + B$

6. $80 \times 40 = 3000 + B$

7. $5 \times 5 \times 5 \times 5 \times 5 = 125 \times B$

8. $4 \times 250 = 1000 + B$

9. $8 \times \$1.25 = B$

10. $\$10.00 = \$8.88 + B$

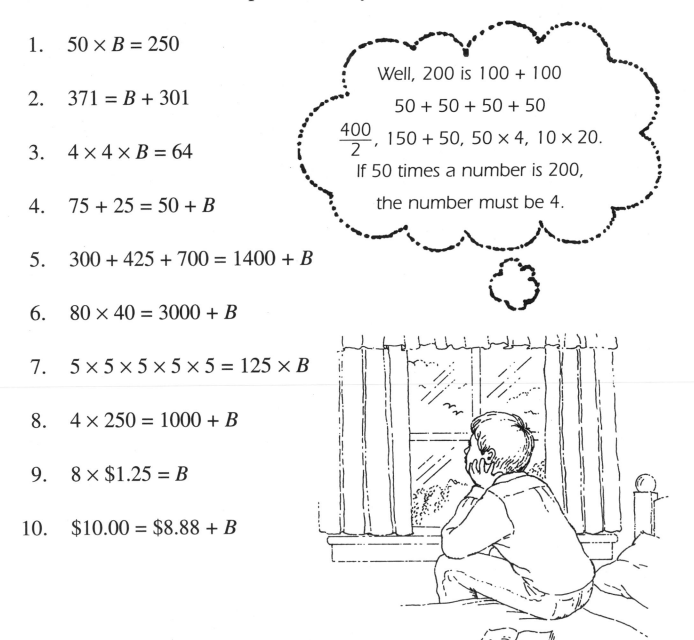

Well, 200 is 100 + 100
50 + 50 + 50 + 50
$\frac{400}{2}$, 150 + 50, 50 × 4, 10 × 20.
If 50 times a number is 200,
the number must be 4.

Thinking About Numbers

Think about each equation. Then, use what you know about numbers to find the value of *C*. Tell what representation you used.

1. $50 + 50 + 75 + 25 = 125 + 3C$

2. $25 \times 4 = 4C + 80$

3. $30 \times 6 = 6 \times (5 + C)$

4. $99 \times 8 = 800 - C$

5. $1000 + C = 2 \times 510$

6. $400 \times 7 = 3000 - C$

7. $2 \times C - 50 = 1400 - 50$

8. $6 \times C + 1 = 4800 + 1$

9. $2 \times \$3.99 = \$5.00 + C$

10. $\$20.00 - 4 \times \$4.99 = C$

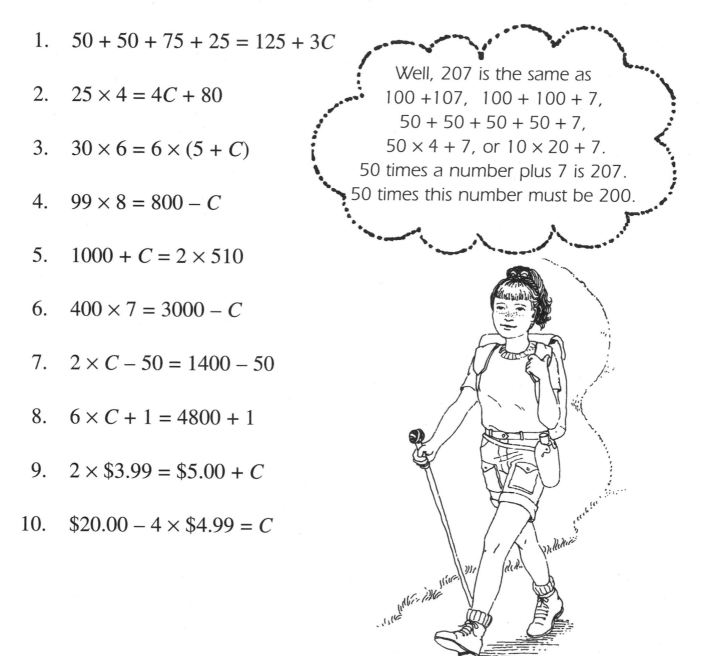

Well, 207 is the same as
100 + 107, 100 + 100 + 7,
50 + 50 + 50 + 50 + 7,
50 × 4 + 7, or 10 × 20 + 7.
50 times a number plus 7 is 207.
50 times this number must be 200.

Thinking About Numbers

Think about each equation. Then, use what you know about numbers to find the value of *D*. Tell what representation you used.

1. If $8 \times 5 = D \times 2 \times 4 \times 5$, then $D =$

2. If $16 \times 5 \times 8 \times D = 0$, then $D =$

3. If $4 = 80 \div D$, then $D =$

4. If $0 = 5 \times 100 - 100D$, then $D =$

5. If $4 \times 80 = 40 \times D$, then $D =$

6. If $2 \times 25 \times 2 = 90 + D$, then $D =$

7. If $2 + D = 2 \times D$, then $D =$

8. If $9 + D = 2 \times D$, then $D =$

9. If $6 + D = 3 \times D$, then $D =$

10. If $10 + D = 3 \times D$, then $D =$

6×4 is $48 \div D$
6×4 is 24,
so $48 \div D$ is 24,
so *D* must be 2.

EXPERIENCE 27

Thinking About Equations

Number Sense Focus

- Multiple representation
- Mental computation

Number Focus

- Activities 1, 2: Whole numbers

Mathematical Background

These activities continue to promote and encourage algebraic thinking by extending the ideas in Experience 26 to multistep equations. For example, $4 \times \text{✽} + 9 = 89$ is a multistep relationship that can be solved mentally: $89 = 80 + 9$, so $4 \times \text{✽}$ must be 80, and since $4 \times 20 = 80$, the ✽ must represent 20.

Using the Activities

1. As a warm-up, you might begin by asking, What are some values the expression $10 \times E + 5$ can represent? Make a list of students' ideas. For example:

    - "If $E = 2$, then it is 25."

    - "If $E = 20$, then it is 205."

    - "If $E = 5$, then it is 55."

    Then, ask: Suppose you knew that $10 \times E + 5 = 85$. How would you decide what E represents?

2. Each activity begins by illustrating multiple representations. As students think about the opening equation, encourage them to describe the thinking that is illustrated and other thinking strategies that lead to a solution.

3. In each activity, show each equation and ask how the value of the variable might be found.

Solutions

Activity 1

1. 300
2. 150
3. 80
4. 1
5. 200

Activity 2

1. 100
2. 10
3. 10
4. 2
5. 1

Extending the Activities

- Have students make up equations, "hide" one of the values by making it a variable, and share their equations with other students.

Thinking About Equations

$660 = 3 \times \square + 60$
660 is 60 + 3 times
a number, so
3 times the number
is 600.
The number is 200.

Try to solve these equations in your head.

1. If $4 \times 80 = \square + 20$, then $\square =$

2. If $150 + 300 = 3 \times \square$, then $\square =$

3. If $4 \times 80 = 400 - \square$, then $\square =$

4. If $80 + 80 \times \square = 160$, then $\square =$

5. If $\square + 400 = 3 \times \square$, then $\square =$

Thinking About Equations

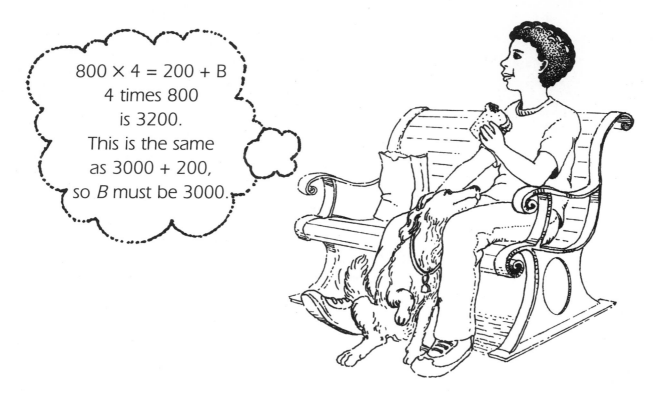

800 × 4 = 200 + B
4 times 800
is 3200.
This is the same
as 3000 + 200,
so *B* must be 3000.

Try to solve these equations in your head.

1. If $400 + (2 \times B) = 600$, then $B =$

2. If $800 + 80 \times B = 1600$, then $B =$

3. If $10,000 - (200 \times B) = 8000$, then $B =$

4. If $(800 + 600) \div B = 700$, then $B =$

5. If $(600 \times 5) \times B = 3000$, then $B =$

Exploring Number Relationships

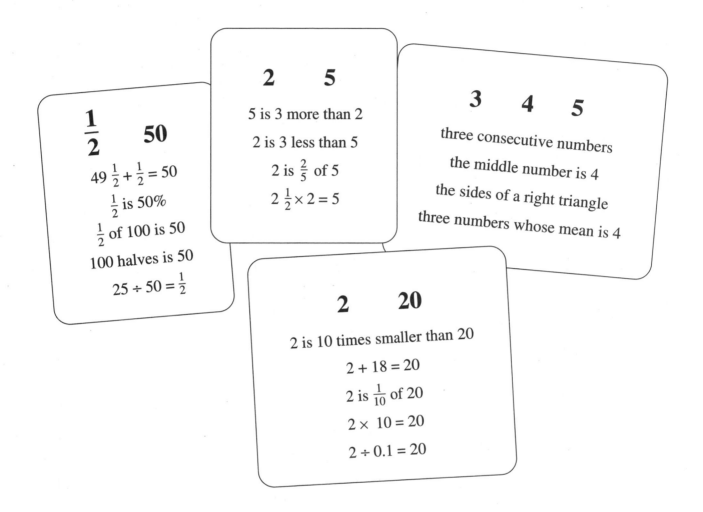

Every number is related to other numbers in many ways. The recognition of multiple relationships among numbers is one of the hallmarks of people with good number sense.

Recognizing relationships between numbers often makes a calculation simpler. For example, we can reason about 19×8 in many ways:

- $8 = 2 \times 2 \times 2$, so $19 \times 8 = 19 \times 2 \times 2 \times 2$, which is the same as double 19 to get 38, then double 38 to get 76, then double 76 to get 152.

- $19 = 20 - 1$, so $19 \times 8 = 20 \times 8 - 1 \times 8 = 160 - 8 = 152$.

- $19 = 10 + 9$, so $19 \times 8 = 10 \times 8 + 9 \times 8 = 80 + 72 = 152$.

The greater the number of relationships among numbers that a person recognizes, the more choices that person has available for mental computation or estimation.

In mental computation, the numbers 10 or 100 are useful, as are compatible numbers and other number relationships. For example, noticing the relationship between each fraction and $\frac{1}{2}$ makes it possible to estimate $\frac{3}{7} + \frac{4}{9}$ as less than 1 easily and confidently. Relationships also exist among sequences of numbers. For example, 1, 1, 2, 3, 5, 8, 13, . . . and 3, 6, 12, 24, 48, . . . are two forms of growth that demonstrate regular relationships between successive numbers in a sequence. Recognizing such patterns helps us to identify trends and regularities in data and to notice when a number seems to be out of place because it does not fit the pattern.

These activities encourage students to explore number relationships and to take advantage of the relationships they observe.

Finding Fractions

Number Sense Focus

- Number relationships
- Relative size

Number Focus

- Activities 1, 2: Fractions

Mathematical Background

Recognizing and correctly naming fractional parts is an important skill. Realizing that $\frac{1}{2}$ of $\frac{1}{2}$ is $\frac{1}{4}$, for example, is an important stage in understanding the concept of $\frac{1}{4}$ and how it relates to $\frac{1}{2}$. Visual representations of fractions can encourage the use of logical relationships in correctly naming fractional parts.

Using the Activities

1. In Activity 1, have students name the fractional part represented by the shaded area of the figure and share their thinking. Encourage the use of logical relationships. For example, in part 1, students might make these observations:

   - "I know that $\frac{1}{4}$ of 1 is $\frac{1}{4}$. And $\frac{1}{4}$ of *this* fourth is $\frac{1}{16}$."

   - "The shaded area is $\frac{1}{4}$ of the smaller square. It takes four smaller squares to make the whole, so it is 1 out of 16, or $\frac{1}{16}$."

   In part 2, the side of the interior square is $\frac{1}{3}$ the side of the exterior square, so the total area is $\frac{1}{9}$. This relationship may not be immediately obvious to the students; accept their conjectures and use them to explore other possibilities.

2. In Activity 2, several parts of each figure are shaded. Ask students to describe how they determined the fractions.

Solutions

Activity 1

1. $\frac{1}{16}$

2. $\frac{1}{9}$

3. $\frac{1}{8}$

4. $\frac{1}{4}$

Activity 2

1. $\frac{1}{18}, \frac{2}{9}, \frac{3}{18}$ (or $\frac{1}{6}$)

2. $\frac{1}{16}, \frac{1}{4}, \frac{1}{8}$

Extending the Activities

• Give students the actual area of one of the shaded regions and ask for the area of the entire figure.

• Name the area of a figure as a certain number of units (say 60 square units), and ask students for the area of the shaded region.

• Present this problem: If the side length of one square is double the side length of another square, how do the areas compare? What about when one side is half the length of the side of the other square? triple the length?

Finding Fractions

1. What fraction of the large square is shaded?

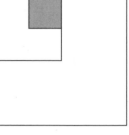

2. What fraction of the large square is shaded?

3. What fraction of the large square is shaded?

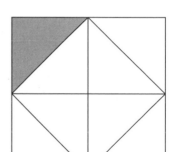

4. What fraction of the large triangle is shaded?

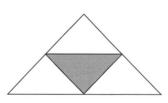

Finding Fractions

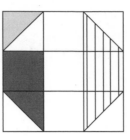

1. What fraction of the large square is shaded ?

    What fraction is shaded ⊞ ?

    What fraction is shaded ▨ ?

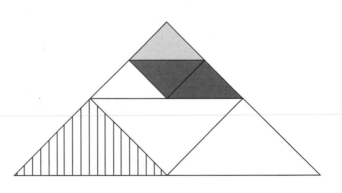

2. What fraction of the large triangle is shaded ▨ ?

    What fraction is shaded ⊞ ?

    What fraction is shaded ▨ ?

Consecutive Numbers

Number Sense Focus

- Number relationships
- Mental computation

Number Focus

- Activities 1–3: Whole numbers

Mathematical Background

Page numbers in books and dates on calendars are examples of consecutive numbers that we encounter daily. The relationships found in consecutive numbers offer interesting and challenging ways to encourage students to think about numbers.

Using the Activities

Although much of the required computation can be done mentally, calculators are a natural tool for exploring the relationships and patterns in these activities.

1. As a warm-up, have students open a book and inspect its page numbers. Establish that numbers following one another in order are called *consecutive numbers*. Make a list of several pairs of consecutive numbers from facing pages in a book. Discuss any patterns or relationships students see in the list.

2. The questions in each activity lend themselves to small-group exploration followed by a class sharing of solutions. If you use them this way, make paper copies of the activities for small groups to use.

Solutions

Activity 1

1. 141
2. 145

3. 153
4. The sums of consecutive pairs differ by 4. Facing pages contains one even and one odd number, so the sum will always be odd.
5. The sum will be even if the first page number is odd, and odd if the first page number is even.
6. 100, 101, 102
7. $148 + 149 + 150 = 447$
8. The sum will always be even, because the sum of two odd and two even numbers is even.
9. Possible answer: $4 \times 70 + 1 + 2 + 3$
10. Possible answer: Use $4 \times n + 1 + 2 + 3$, where n is the first of the four numbers.

Activity 2

1. 110
2. 156
3. The products are all even numbers, because the product of an even and an odd number is even.
4. The products are all even numbers, because the product of two even and one odd number, or of two odd and one even number, is even. They are also all divisible by 6.
5. 00; Possible explanation: the factors $2 \times 5 \times 10$; or 10×20 will give products ending in two zeros.

Activity 3

1. 0, 1, and 2 (not necessarily in that order)
2. The remainders are always 0, 1, and 2, but the order depends on the numbers chosen.
3. The remainders are always 0, 1, 2, and 3.
4. Possible answer: 13, 14, 15, 16, 17; I found a multiple of 5 and then added 3. This number, 13, is the first of the five numbers.
5. 0, 1, 2, 3, 4, and 5; Explanations will vary.

Extending the Activities

• •

- Have students make up a problem involving consecutive numbers and explain how they constructed their problem.

- Ask students to find the number of zeros in the product of 50 consecutive pages, from page 1 to page 50.

- Ask: If you multiply any three consecutive numbers, will the product always be divisible by 6? Why or why not? What can you find out about the product of any four consecutive numbers?

- Ask: If you multiply all the page numbers from 1 to 100, how many zeros will be at the end of the product? *(21, the eleven zeros at the ends of the factors 10, 20, . . . , 100 and the ten zeros from the ten factors of 5 and as many factors of 2)*

Consecutive Numbers

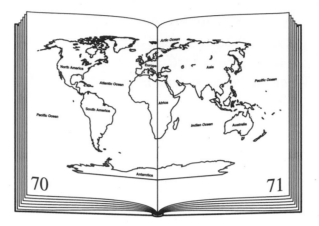

1. What is the sum of these two facing pages?

2. Suppose you turn the page. What is the sum of the new facing pages?

3. You turn the page twice more. What is the sum of the facing pages?

4. What patterns do you see in these sums? Why is every sum of facing page numbers an odd number?

5. Find the sum of three consecutive page numbers. When will the sum be even?

6. If the sum of three consecutive pages is 303, what are the three pages? How did you find them?

7. If the last page of a book is 150, what is the sum of the last three pages?

8. Find the sum of four consecutive page numbers. Will the sum of any four consecutive pages be even or odd? Explain.

9. How can you use the number 70 to find the sum of page numbers 70, 71, 72, and 73?

10. How can you use the method you used in part 9 to find the sum of any four consecutive pages?

Number SENSE / Grades 6–8

Consecutive Numbers

1. What is the product of these two facing pages?

2. Suppose you turn the page. What is the product of the new facing pages?

3. Find the products of five different pairs of consecutive pages. What do you notice about the products? Can you explain what you see?

4. Find the products of five different sets of *three* consecutive pages. What do you notice about the products? Tell why.

5. If you multiply every page number in this book, what will the last two digits of the product be? How do you know?

Consecutive Numbers

1. Choose any two facing pages in a book and the next page. Divide each page number by 3. What are the remainders?

2. Choose any three consecutive numbers. Divide each number by 3, and record the remainders. Do this for other sets of three consecutive numbers. What do you notice about the remainders?

3. Choose four consecutive numbers. Divide each number by 4, and record the remainders. Repeat this with other sets of four consecutive numbers. What do you notice about the remainders?

4. Find five consecutive numbers that, when divided by 5, give remainders of 3, 4, 0, 1, and 2—in that order. Explain how you did it.

5. Choose six consecutive numbers. Predict what the remainders will be when each number is divided by 6, then check your prediction. What do you find?

Meeting Conditions

Number Sense Focus

- Number relationships
- Multiple representation

Number Focus

- Activities 1 and 2: Whole numbers
- Activity 3: Decimals

Mathematical Background

Numbers can be classified in endless ways—according to magnitude, proximity to other numbers, factors, and so forth. In these activities, students are encouraged to examine the properties of numbers they see every day and to create numbers satisfying certain conditions.

Using the Activities

1. As a warm-up, write a three-digit number on the board, and ask the class to state as many properties as possible about that number. Ask questions to encourage them. Is it odd or even? What are its divisors? Is it less than 1000? greater than 99?

2. Activity 1 may be done with pages torn from a telephone book rather than with the numbers on the activity sheet. Verify that students understand that more than one number may fit each category. Encourage them to use divisibility rules when convenient (for example, if the sum of the digits is divisible by 3, the number is also).

3. In Activity 2, make sure students realize that 12:36 means 36 minutes past 12 and is not really the same as the number 1236. Check that they understand that certain numbers—such as 0660, 0575, and 3200—are not acceptable clock numbers. Ask students to predict—without actually dividing—which numbers from 1 to 9 will evenly divide the number shown on the clock, 1236. (1, 2, 3, 4, and 6) Have them share how they

made their predictions. Encourage them to make organized lists when identifying consecutive clock numbers.

4. In Activity 3, remind students that an odometer registers the kilometers or miles that have been traveled. Be sure students realize that the last digit in an odometer displays tenths. Ask whether the odometer is showing miles or kilometers. For example, you might ask: What will be the next value shown? *(99.6)* How much further have you traveled? *(0.1)* (*We can't tell from the information given.*) If necessary, help students understand the questions. For example, to find how far the car must travel to have a certain odometer reading, students must first determine what the reading will be.

Solutions

Activity 1

1. 9979
2. 1001
3. 9876
4. 9505
5. 4500, 4511, 4512, 4848, 4879, and 4935
6. 3030 and 4500
7. 4500, 4512, and 4848
8. 1001, 4500, 4511, 4512, 4935, 6400, 7362, 8761, 9505, 9876, 9979
9. 1001
10. 4500, 4512

Activity 2

1. 2359 (24-hour clock), 1259 (12-hour clock)
2. 0100
3. any clock number ending 00 or 50
4. 720, 726, 732, 738, 744, and 750
5. any clock number ending in 0
6. 24
7. 24 (The first 12 are 120, 240, 300, 420, 540, 600, 720, 840, 900, 1020, 1140, 1200)
8. 118 or 779 (depending on the clock)
9. 4 times (12-hour clock), 3 times (24-hour clock: 0123, 1234, 2345)

Activity 3

1. One possible answer is 111011.6 which produces all ones.
2. 0.5 (Even numbers must be whole numbers.)
3. 300.5
4. 2.5
5. 19950.5
6. 279900.5
7. 999900.4

Extending the Activities

- Present this challenge: Find any four-digit number that is divisible by 3. Now, form a second four-digit number from these same digits. Is this number divisible by 3? Form a third four-digit number from the same digits, if possible. Is it also divisible by 3? Explain what you observe.

- Have students list five properties of the number formed by the last four digits of their telephone number.

- Have students investigate and report on properties of other everyday numbers, such as numbers in addresses and on license plates.

Meeting Conditions

Hmmm, let's see. There's...

555-1565	555-3030	555-4356
555-4848	555-6400	555-2346
555-4879	555-4935	555-1234
555-4512	555-9979	555-4500
555-7362	555-5678	555-4511
555-5675	555-1001	555-8761
555-9505	555-9876	

From this list of telephone numbers, find one or more numbers with each of the following properties. Use only the last four digits.

1. It is the greatest 4-digit number.   2. It is the least 4-digit number.

3. It is the greatest even number.   4. It is the greatest multiple of 5.

5. It is between 4500 and 5000.   6. It is divisible by 2, 3, and 5.

7. It is a multiple of 4 between and including 4500 and 5000.

8. It has more thousands than tens.

9. It has a remainder of 1 when divided by 1000.

10. Write the smallest and largest 4-digit number that meets the conditions in 7 and 8.

Meeting Conditions

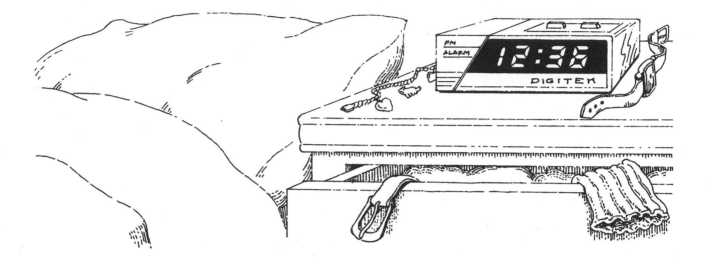

In 1–5, find "clock numbers" that meet the given condition.

1. It is the greatest clock number.

2. It is the least clock number.

3. It is a multiple of 50.

4. It is a multiple of 6 between 720 and 750.

5. It is divisible by 2 and 5.

How many times a day does the clock show

6. numbers divisible by 100?

7. numbers divisible by 60?

8. numbers greater than 1200?

9. consecutive digits, such as 1234?

10. List three conditions or properties about a number that is showing on a digital clock right now.

Meeting Conditions

0	0	0	0	9	9	5

How far will this car have to travel before the odometer shows

1. a number with all the same digits?

2. an even number?

3. a number with 4 in the hundreds place?

4. a whole number evenly divisible by 3?

5. a number greater than 20,000 and divisible by 50?

6. a number between 250,000 and 300,000 and divisible by 70,000?

7. the largest number that can be shown on the odometer?

In 8–10, write an odometer reading that

8. is greater than 500,000.

9. is a multiple of 50.

10. is a string of 7 consecutive digits.

Where on the Number Line?

Number Sense Focus

- Number relationships
- Mental computation

Number Focus

- Activity 1: Fractions
- Activities 2, 3: Fractions, decimals

Mathematical Background

The continuous nature of the number line challenges students to examine the notion of "betweenness" and to think about and explore number relationships. For example, some of the same techniques useful for finding a point between $\frac{1}{2}$ and 1 can be applied to finding a point between $\frac{4}{7}$ and $\frac{5}{7}$, but students often find the latter problem much more challenging.

Using the Activities

1. As a warm-up, lead students through this activity:

   - Draw a number line across a page and mark the endpoints 0 and 1.

   - Fold the number line in half, unfold it, and label the halfway point. ($\frac{1}{2}$)

   - Fold the number line in half again, unfold it, and label the new folds. ($\frac{1}{4}$ *and* $\frac{3}{4}$)

   - Repeat this twice more. What would you mark the new folds? ($\frac{1}{8}, \frac{3}{8}, \frac{5}{8},$ *and* $\frac{7}{8};$ $\frac{1}{16}, \frac{3}{16}, \frac{5}{16}, \frac{7}{16}, \frac{9}{16}, \frac{11}{16}, \frac{13}{16}, \frac{15}{16}$)

   - Describe any patterns you see.

   - Locate a fraction on your number line that is *not* on a fold.

   - If you continued to fold your number line as we have been doing, would the fraction you named eventually be on a fold? Why or why not?

2. Show the illustration at the top of Activity 1. The circular regions are fraction models that help connect the symbolic representation to the number line. Ask students to match each circular model with one of the fractions shown and to tell how they matched them. Then, ask where each fraction should be placed on the number line. Once the fractions have been placed, have students explain how they decided where each belonged.

3. In the activity, discuss which fraction goes with which fraction card and where each fraction card belongs on the number line.

4. Follow a similar procedure in Activities 2 and 3.

Extending the Activities

- Ask students to draw other number lines with endpoints of 0 and 1, and fold them repeatedly—for example, into thirds repeatedly—labeling the fold points.

Where on the Number Line?

Decide about where each fraction belongs on the number line.

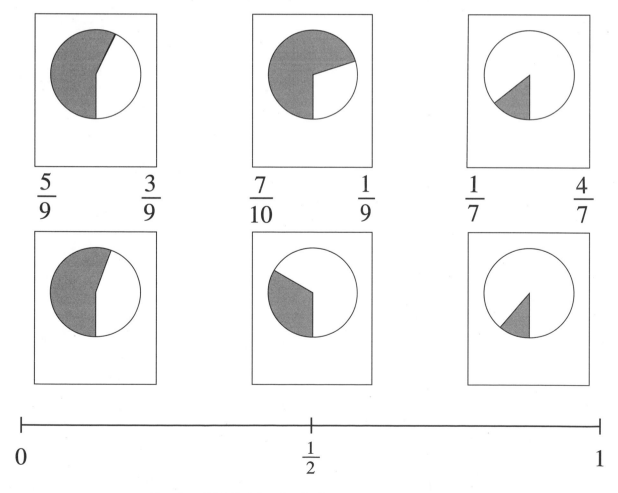

$$\frac{5}{9} \qquad \frac{3}{9}$$

$$\frac{7}{10} \qquad \frac{1}{9}$$

$$\frac{1}{7} \qquad \frac{4}{7}$$

$$0 \qquad\qquad \frac{1}{2} \qquad\qquad 1$$

Where on the Number Line?

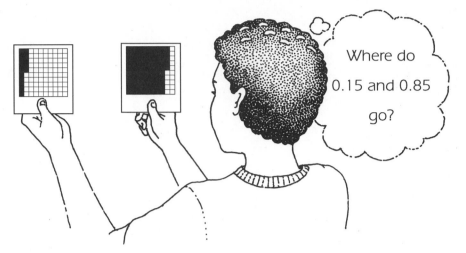

Where do 0.15 and 0.85 go?

Decide about where each decimal belongs on the number line.

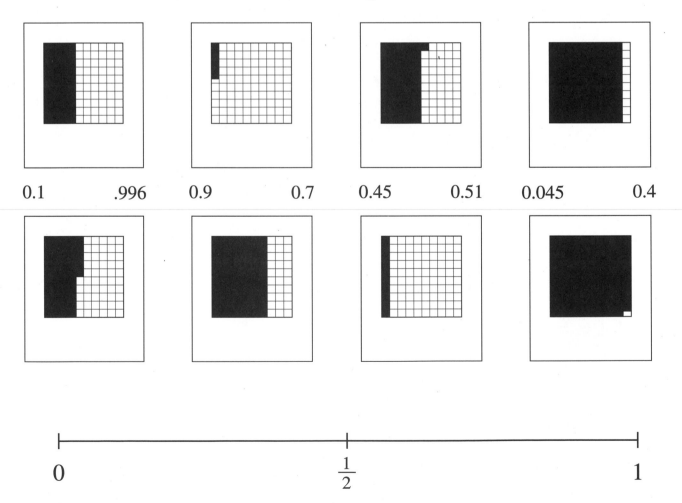

0.1 .996	0.9 0.7	0.45 0.51	0.045 0.4

0         $\frac{1}{2}$ 1

Where on the Number Line?

Where do 0.15 and $\frac{6}{7}$ go?

Decide about where each fraction belongs on the number line.

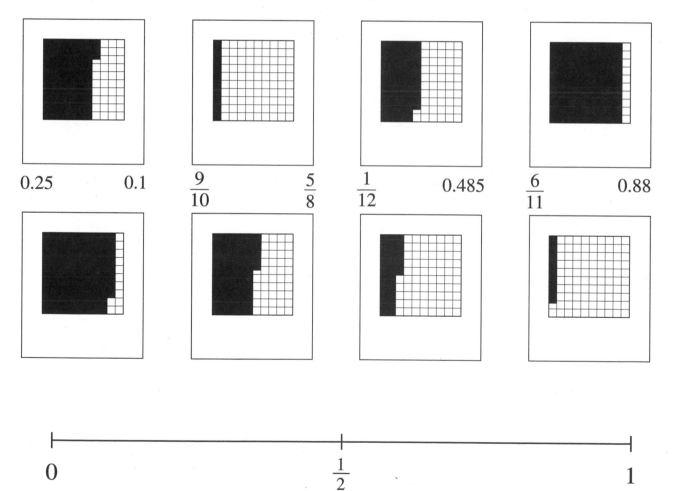

0.25   0.1 $\frac{9}{10}$ $\frac{5}{8}$ $\frac{1}{12}$ 0.485 $\frac{6}{11}$ 0.88

0 $\frac{1}{2}$ 1

EXPERIENCE 32

....

Patterns on Number Lines

Number Sense Focus

- Number relationships
- Mental computation

Number Focus

- Activity 1: Fractions
- Activity 2: Decimals
- Activity 3: Fractions, decimals

Mathematical Background

....

Arranging the values in sequences along number lines encourages students to take advantage of benchmarks. For example, in placing $\frac{3}{7}$ and $\frac{4}{7}$ along a number line, knowing that $\frac{3}{7}$ is slightly less than $\frac{1}{2}$ and that $\frac{4}{7}$ is slightly greater than $\frac{1}{2}$ helps not only to order the fractions but to place them in their approximate positions.

Using the Activities

....

In these activities, students use known benchmarks to place fractions and decimals along a number line.

1. In each activity, have students complete the sequence and then indicate the position of some of the points along the number line. The points they choose to locate will give you insight into how they are using benchmarks.

2. Use Activities 2 and 3 in a similar way. All of the sequences follow a simple rule; they are a single sequence. Encourage students to explain how they determined the missing values. If they are having difficulty, ask whether showing all the values as decimals or as fractions helps.

Solutions

Activity 1

1. $\frac{4}{10}, \frac{5}{10}, \frac{6}{10}, \frac{7}{10}$

2. $\frac{5}{8}, \frac{6}{8}, \frac{7}{8}, \frac{8}{8}$

3. $\frac{1}{16}, \frac{1}{32}, \frac{1}{64}, \frac{1}{128}$

4. $\frac{12}{4}, \frac{15}{4}, \frac{18}{4}, \frac{21}{4}$

Activity 2

1. 3.0, 3.5, 4.0

2. 2.7, 3.0, 3.3

3. 1.5, 1.8, 2.1

4. 1.6, 3.2, 6.4

Activity 3

The answer may take different correct forms. Here are some possibilities.

1. 0.75, $\frac{9}{10}$, 1.05, $\frac{6}{5}$

2. 0.625, $\frac{3}{4}$, 0.875, 1

3. 3.75, $4\frac{1}{2}$, 5.25, 6

4. 3.4, $3\frac{4}{5}$, 4.2, $4\frac{3}{5}$

Extending the Activities

• •

- Ask students to mark the endpoints of a line segment with different pairs of numbers and then identify some useful benchmarks.

- Provide a range—say from 2 to 5—and ask students to make a sequence of at least five numbers that satisfies certain conditions, such as all numbers in the sequence fall within that range; or all numbers fall between 3 and 5; or all numbers extend beyond 5.

Patterns on Number Lines

For each pattern, find the next four numbers in the sequence. Then, pick any four numbers in the sequence and show *about* where they go on the number line.

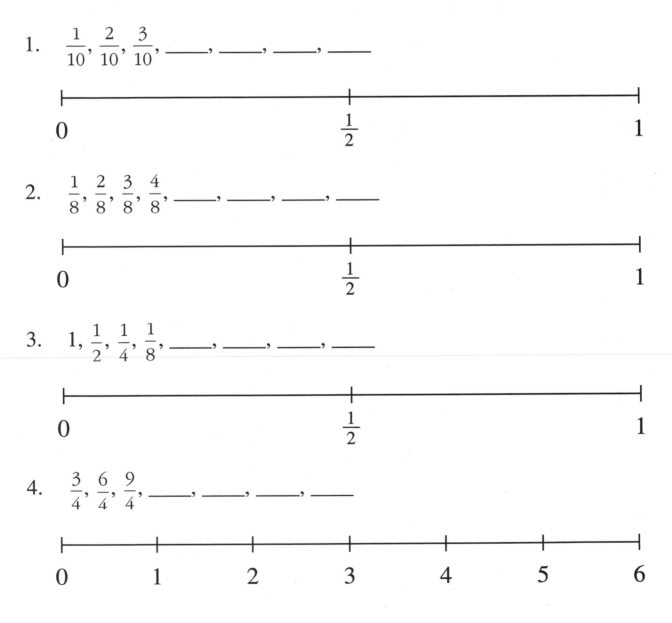

1. $\frac{1}{10}, \frac{2}{10}, \frac{3}{10},$ ____, ____, ____, ____

   0          $\frac{1}{2}$ 1

2. $\frac{1}{8}, \frac{2}{8}, \frac{3}{8}, \frac{4}{8},$ ____, ____, ____, ____

   0          $\frac{1}{2}$ 1

3. $1, \frac{1}{2}, \frac{1}{4}, \frac{1}{8},$ ____, ____, ____, ____

   0          $\frac{1}{2}$ 1

4. $\frac{3}{4}, \frac{6}{4}, \frac{9}{4},$ ____, ____, ____, ____

   0   1   2   3   4   5   6

Number SENSE / Grades 6–8

Patterns on Number Lines

For each pattern, find the next three numbers in the sequence. Then, pick any four numbers in the sequence and show *about* where they go on the number line.

1. 0.5, 1.0, 1.5, 2.0, 2.5, _____, _____, _____

2. 1.2, 1.5, 1.8, 2.1, 2.4, _____, _____, _____

3. 0.3, 0.6, 0.9, 1.2, _____, _____, _____

4. 0.2, 0.4, 0.8, _____, _____, _____

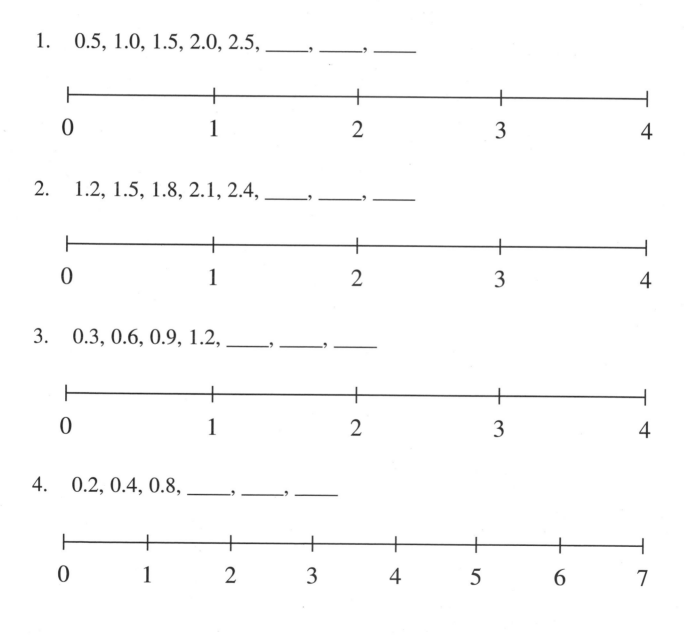

Patterns on Number Lines

For each pattern, find the next four numbers in the sequence. Then, pick any four numbers in the sequence and show *about* where they go on the number line.

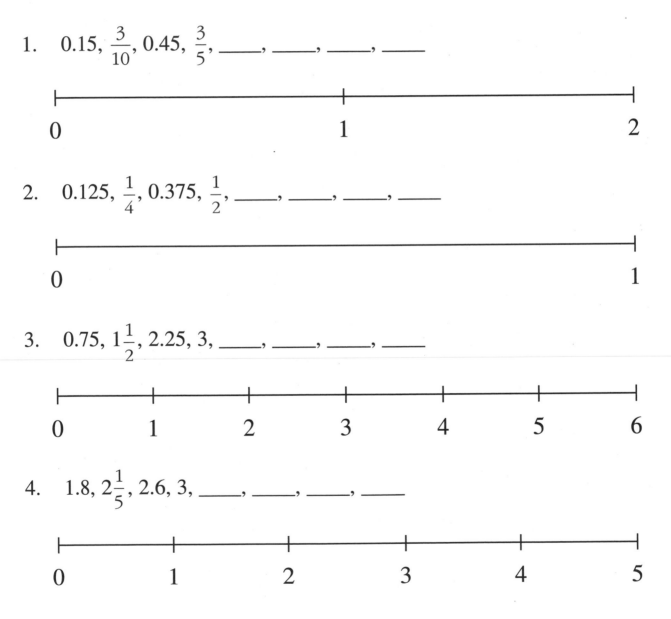

1. 0.15, $\frac{3}{10}$, 0.45, $\frac{3}{5}$, ____, ____, ____, ____

2. 0.125, $\frac{1}{4}$, 0.375, $\frac{1}{2}$, ____, ____, ____, ____

3. 0.75, $1\frac{1}{2}$, 2.25, 3, ____, ____, ____, ____

4. 1.8, $2\frac{1}{5}$, 2.6, 3, ____, ____, ____, ____

. . . .

Name That Decimal

Number Sense Focus

- Number relationships
- Multiple representation

Number Focus

- Activities 1–3: Fractions, decimals

Mathematical Background

. . . .

Part of good number sense is recognizing different ways of expressing numbers and characteristics of those numbers. These activities encourage thoughtful reflection about numbers by giving students a chance to name decimals that satisfy certain clues.

Using the Activities

. . . .

1. As a warm-up, ask students to describe different ways to represent $0.50, such as 50 cents or a half dollar. Make a list of their ideas to demonstrate that there are many such representations. Extend their thinking by providing other clues for representations of $0.50, such as these:

   - It is a coin that is larger than a quarter but worth less than a dollar.

   - Fifty coins of equal value can be used to make it.

   - The coin has a likeness of President Kennedy on its face.

   - Five coins of equal value or ten coins of equal value can be used to make it.

2. Form teams of two to four students. Display Activity 1, or read each set of clues aloud. Ask each team to write one answer for each set of clues. Some clues are extraneous; teams should decide which clues are unnecessary for solving each mystery.

3. Follow a similar procedure for Activities 2 and 3.

Solutions

Activity 1

1. 0.25; Clues a and b
2. 0.55; Clues a, b, c, and d
3. 1.8; Clues a and c
4. 0.55; Clues b, c, and d

Activity 2

1. 0.32; Clues a, b, and c
2. 2.25; Any single clue can be used.
3. 0.51; Clue b
4. 0.96; Clue c

Activity 3

1. 0.3; Clue d
2. $\frac{2}{3}$ or 0.6666 . . .; Clues a and c
3. 0.94; Clue a
4. 0.6; Clues a, c, and d

Extending the Activities

- Have teams create Mystery Number problems and exchange them with other teams.

- Ask each team to prepare a list of clues for a given decimal. Make a master list of all the clues, and discuss similarities and differences between the clues the teams developed.

Name That Decimal

The Mystery Decimal . . .	Solution

1. *Clue a:* is greater than 0.2

   Clue b: is less than $\frac{3}{10}$

   Clue c: is halfway between 0.2 and 0.3

   Mystery Decimal _____

   Unnecessary clues _____

2. *Clue a:* is between 0.4 and 0.6

   Clue b: is greater than one half

   Clue c: is less than 1

   Clue d: has two decimal places

   Clue e: is 5 hundredths less than 6 tenths

   Mystery Decimal _____

   Unnecessary clues _____

3. *Clue a:* is less than 3

   Clue b: is twice 0.9

   Clue c: is more than one half

   Mystery Decimal _____

   Unnecessary clues _____

4. *Clue a:* is 3 tenths more than $\frac{1}{4}$

   Clue b: is more than one half

   Clue c: is between 0.5 and 0.6

   Clue d: is less than 1

   Mystery Decimal _____

   Unnecessary clues _____

Name That Decimal

The Mystery Decimal . . .	Solution

1. *Clue a:* is greater than $\frac{1}{4}$

   Clue b: is less than $\frac{1}{3}$

   Clue c: is less than two fifths

   Clue d: is two hundredths more than 0.3

   Mystery Decimal _____

   Unnecessary clues _____

2. *Clue a:* is three times 0.75

   Clue b: is 1.25 more than 2

   Clue c: is 0.25 less than 2.5

   Mystery Decimal _____

   Unnecessary clues _____

3. *Clue a:* is between $\frac{2}{5}$ and $\frac{5}{8}$

   Clue b: is less than 1

   Clue c: is within exactly 0.11 of two fifths

   Mystery Decimal _____

   Unnecessary clues _____

4. *Clue a:* is more than $\frac{4}{5}$

   Clue b: is a multiple of 0.32

   Clue c: is more than one half

   Clue d: is less than 1

   Mystery Decimal _____

   Unnecessary clues _____

Name That Decimal

The Mystery Decimal . . .   **Solution**

1. *Clue a:* when multiplied by 10 gives
      a whole number   Mystery Decimal _____
   Clue b: is between but excluding   Unnecessary clues _____
      0.2 and 0.6
   Clue c: is closer to $\frac{1}{4}$ than one half
   Clue d: when doubled is less than one

2. *Clue a:* is less than one   Mystery Decimal _____
   Clue b: is either $\frac{2}{3}$ or $\frac{6}{7}$ Unnecessary clues _____
   Clue c: is more than one half
   Clue d: is between 0.6 and 0.7

3. *Clue a:* is less than one   Mystery Decimal _____
   Clue b: is exactly 0.04 from $\frac{9}{10}$ Unnecessary clues _____
   Clue c: is more than $\frac{8}{9}$

4. *Clue a:* is less than $\frac{8}{11}$ Mystery Decimal _____
   Clue b: is within 0.10 of 0.65   Unnecessary clues _____
   Clue c: is more than one half
   Clue d: is less than 1
   Clue e: is equivalent to $\frac{2}{5}$, $\frac{3}{5}$, or $\frac{4}{5}$

EXPERIENCE 34

Which Is the Greatest?

Number Sense Focus

- Number relationships
- Relative size

Number Focus

- Activities 1–3: Decimals

Mathematical Background

Early experiences with whole-number multiplication involve products larger than either factor. When one factor is between 0 and 1, the product is always less than the other factor. An understanding of this relationship takes time to develop. Calculators are a natural tool for exploring this relationship. However, many comparisons can be made without actual computations. These activities reward such thinking.

Using the Activities

1. As a warm-up to Activity 1, have students enter any decimal less than 1 into a calculator and multiply it by 25. Make a list of their decimals and products. For example:

Enter	Result	Enter	Result
0.8	20	0.91	22.75
0.9	22.5	0.99	24.75

   Ask students what patterns they notice in their results. *(The product is always less than the factor 25, and the closer the decimal is to 1, the closer the product is to 25.)*

2. In Activity 1, students determine which product is the greatest in each set. Ask which products they need to compute and which can be decided in other ways. For example, 40×0.8 is greater than 40×0.75 and 40×0.666 because they have a common factor (40) and 0.8 is the greatest decimal of the three decimals.

3. As a warm-up to Activity 2, have students enter any decimal greater than 1 into a calculator and multiply it by 25. Make a list of their results. For example:

Enter	Result	Enter	Result
2.74	68.5	1.02	25.5
1.8	45	1.002	25.05
1.2	30		

Ask what patterns they notice. (*The product is always more than the factor 25, and the closer the decimal is to 1, the closer the product is to 25.*)

4. As a warm-up to Activity 3, have students multiply several decimals near but less than $\frac{1}{2}$, and several near but greater than $\frac{1}{2}$, by 25. List their results. For example:

Enter	Result	Enter	Result
0.44	11	0.51	12.75
0.48	12	0.52	13
0.49	12.25	0.56	14

Ask what patterns they notice. (*One pattern is that the product of a decimal near $\frac{1}{2}$ is nearly half the other factor.*)

Solutions

Activity 1	Activity 2	Activity 3
1. 40×0.8	1. 40×1.8	1. 73×0.51
2. 73×0.9	2. 73×2.1	2. 20×0.49
3. 20×0.91	3. 20×1.1	3. 40×0.54
4. 80×0.910	4. 80×1.22	4. 80×0.49
5. 54×0.9	5. 54×1.05	5. 54×0.55
6. 60×0.9	6. $60 \times 1.2 \times 1.2$	6. 60×0.5
7. 60×0.6	7. 60×1.8	7. $60 \times 0.51 \times 0.51$
8. 40×0.9	8. 80×0.6	8. 40×0.51
9. $70 \times 0.8 \times 0.8$	9. $70 \times 1.5 \times 1.5$	9. 70×0.48
10. 80×0.99	10. 80×1.01	10. 80×0.49

Extending the Activities

• •

- Ask students to make up a computation problem in which the product is near one of the factors. Then have them make up a problem in which the product is near half of one factor. Have them explain how they constructed their problems.

Which Is the Greatest?

In each set, decide which product is the greatest. Explain how you know.

1. 40×0.8 40×0.75 40×0.666

2. 73×0.9 73×0.7 73×0.8

3. 20×0.900 20×0.90 20×0.91

4. 80×0.901 80×0.910 80×0.9

5. 54×0.89 54×0.9 54×0.777

6. 60×0.9 60×0.8 $60 \times 0.9 \times 0.9$

7. 30×0.81 60×0.4 60×0.6

8. 40×0.9 40×0.6 80×0.3

9. $70 \times 0.8 \times 0.8$ 70×0.6 70×0.54

10. 80×0.9009 80×0.909 80×0.99

Which Is the Greatest?

In each set, decide which product is the greatest. Explain how you know.

1. 40×1.8 40×1.08 40×0.8

2. 73×2.1 73×1.2 73×1.89

3. 20×1.01 20×1.1 20×0.91

4. 80×1.21 80×1.12 80×1.22

5. 54×1.039 54×1.05 54×1.03

6. 60×1.2 60×1.4 $60 \times 1.2 \times 1.2$

7. 30×1.7 60×1.8 60×1.755

8. 40×1.05 40×1.1 80×0.6

9. $70 \times 1.5 \times 1.5$ 70×1.9 70×1.995

10. 80×1.002 80×1.01 80×1.0095

Which Is the Greatest?

In each set, decide which product is the greatest. Explain how you know.

1. 73×0.493 73×0.4559 73×0.51

2. 20×0.44 20×0.49 20×0.478

3. 40×0.54 40×0.48 40×0.444

4. 80×0.49 80×0.488 80×0.48

5. 54×0.55 54×0.47 54×0.532

6. $60 \times 0.5 \times 0.5$ 60×0.4 60×0.5

7. 30×0.51 $60 \times 0.51 \times 0.51$ $60 \times 0.51 \times 0.51 \times 0.51$

8. 40×0.51 40×0.5 80×0.25

9. 70×0.47 $70 \times 0.47 \times 0.47$ 70×0.48

10. 80×0.49 $80 \times 0.5 \times 0.5$ $80 \times 0.5 \times 0.5 \times 0.5$

Exploring Reasonableness

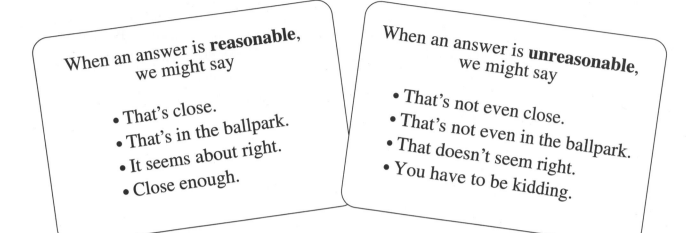

When an answer is **reasonable**, we might say

- That's close.
- That's in the ballpark.
- It seems about right.
- Close enough.

When an answer is **unreasonable**, we might say

- That's not even close.
- That's not even in the ballpark.
- That doesn't seem right.
- You have to be kidding.

Assessing whether computational results are reasonable is an important decision-making process that requires sensitivity to the operations and the numbers involved. Consider these results:

A.	289	B.	289	C.	289	D.	289	E.	289	F.	289
	× 3		× 3		× 3		× 3		× 3		× 3
	1067		67		868		292		877		907

Recognizing that these results are incorrect requires reflection and analysis. The critical thinking required to assess such answers must be adjusted to fit the situation. The concept of reasonableness, for example, could be used to reject all but one of these results.

If you know the product of two odd numbers must be odd, you could reject the answer to C as being unreasonable, though it is very close to correct. If you reason that $300 \times 3 = 900$, so 289×3 must be less than 900, you could reject the answers to A and F as being unreasonable. Though the answers to B and D are less than 900, they could be rejected because they are not as close to 900 as would be expected.

The answer to E is reasonable but incorrect. Checking for reasonableness only detects answers that are logically incorrect or clearly inappropriate. The answer to E satisfies the tests for reasonableness that were applied above. Thus an answer may be incorrect and still be reasonable.

Reasonableness is difficult to define, but our goal is to encourage inquiry that will help students to think about the numbers, the operation, and the situation, and to make judgments. The more opportunities students have to think about results and the more they are challenged to decide what is reasonable, the more they will come to value the question, "Is this about what I expect?"

What Does the Graph Say?

Number Sense Focus

• Reasonableness

Number Focus

• Activity 1: Whole numbers, percents, fractions

Mathematical Background

• •

Graphs are designed to communicate information quickly, but graphs and other displays of numerical information should be examined carefully, or misinterpretations may result. Sometimes graphs intentionally distort information; one of the most popular ways of misrepresenting information is by manipulating how the axes are scaled and displayed.

Using the Activity

• •

1. Display the headline and the graph, and ask whether students agree with the headline. Is it possible for a newspaper to be biased toward a proposal or candidate? What other conclusions might be drawn from the graph?

2. Have the class examine each of the conclusions. If necessary, ask specific questions to focus students on the labeling of the vertical axis, such as: What percent of people are for the proposal? What is the difference between the percent of people for the proposal and the percent against it? Is this a big difference?

Solutions

All of the conclusions were drawn by comparing only the areas of the bars.

1. This conclusion does not reflect the fact that the percent of people for the proposal (33%) and against it (35%) are very close. This conclusion was drawn by ignoring the labeling of the vertical axis and concluding that twice as many people are against the proposal as are for it, and that the undecided group is too small to make a difference.

2. The graph reports 32% as undecided, not $\frac{1}{7}$.
3. The graph reports 35% against, 33% for the proposal.
4. The sum of these two groups is actually 65%.

Extending the Activity

- Have students construct a graph of this information that gives a more accurate picture of the relative proportions.

- Ask students to search for graphs in newspapers or magazines that they think are misleading or easy to misinterpret.

What Does the Graph Say?

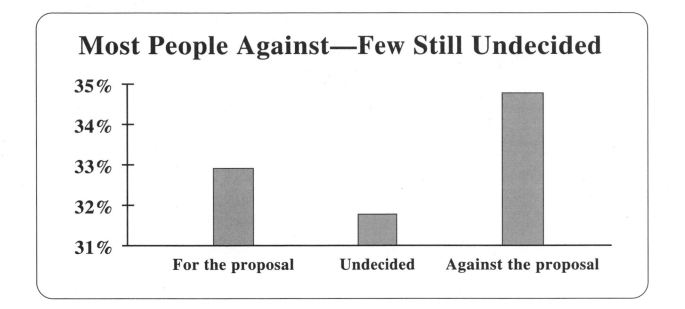

Most People Against—Few Still Undecided

For each conclusion below, answer these questions:
What is wrong with the conclusion?
How might the conclusion have been drawn from the graph?

1. The proposal is doomed to failure.

2. About $\frac{1}{7}$ of people are still undecided.

3. Twice as many people are against the proposal as for it.

4. Even if all those people who are currently undecided vote for the proposal, it still wouldn't pass.

EXPERIENCE 36

How High Is the Stack?

Number Sense Focus

- Reasonableness

Number Focus

- Activity 1: Whole numbers

Mathematical Background

Advertisements are designed to attract attention and to sell products or services. To this end, factually correct data are often manipulated to reflect well on the company placing the ad. Mathematics can help us critically review ads. This activity seeks to help students develop a healthy suspicion for ads and a greater appreciation of the power of mathematics.

Using the Activity

1. Show the advertisement, and ask students to decide what is wrong or misleading about it. (A similar ad was used by a bank to encourage people to seek home improvement loans.) Make sure students share all the ways they are reasoning about the problem.

2. Ask questions to encourage students to look more closely at the advertisement.

    - About how much money is in the stack? (If necessary, ask how tall a stack of 125 $100 bills would be. Students may want to build a paper model.)

    - What is the least amount of money that could be in the stack? *(A $100 bill on top of $1 bills would make the least.)*

    - What is the most amount of money that could be in the stack? *(A $100 bill on top of $100 bills would make the most. The $100 is the largest U.S. bill in circulation today.)*

Solution
The stack seems to be made entirely of $100 bills. But $12,500 requires only 125 bills, which would be much shorter than this stack.

Extending the Activity

• •

- Propose this problem: It was reported that adults have about 4 hours of leisure time per day, and that women have 2 minutes more leisure time per day than men. Show this on a graph (1) that represents the data fairly; (2) that represents the data unfairly. Show your graphs to a few friends, and ask what the graphs tell them.

- Invite students to explore whether $1,000,000 would fit in a suitcase.

How High Is the Stack?

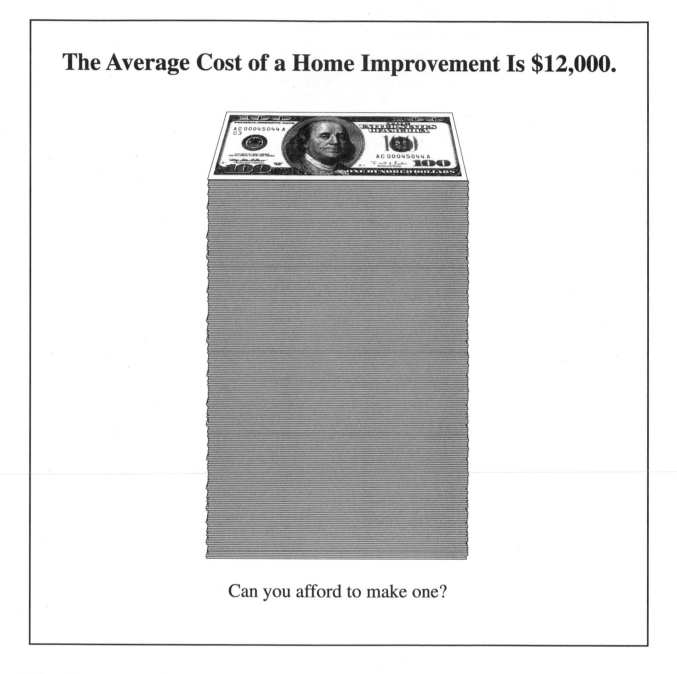

The Average Cost of a Home Improvement Is $12,000.

Can you afford to make one?

What is wrong with this picture?

Odd Result Out

Number Sense Focus

- Reasonableness
- Mental computation

Number Focus

- Activity 1: Whole numbers
- Activity 2: Whole numbers, fractions, decimals

Mathematical Background
••••••••••••••••••••••••••••••

Recognizing when computations produce similar results can be helpful in making estimates, judging the relative size of results, and determining the reasonableness of results. For example, $8 \times 8 \times 24$ is about the same as 60×25 which is about the same as 70×20. Knowing that computational options exist gives students viable alternatives for doing computations and encourages them to think about numbers and ways of working with them.

Using the Activities
•••••••••••••••••••••••••••••

1. As a warm-up, write five values on the board—54,578, 55,000, 50,000, 60,000, and 100,000—and ask, Which of these doesn't belong? Although all of these values might round to 100,000, the 100,000 seems the most different from the others. One might also argue that the precision suggested by 54,578 makes it the most different. Such thoughtful reflection should be encouraged.

2. In each activity, display the set of computations and ask students to share their reasoning about which result doesn't seem to belong.

Solutions

These are possible answers. Explanations will vary.

Activity 1

1. $99 \times 20 + 4$
2. $10 \times 10 \times 3$
3. $48 \times 100 - 100$

Activity 2

1. 100×120
2. $(50 \div \frac{1}{2}) \times (20 \div \frac{1}{2})$
3. $20 \times 30 + 5$

Extending the Activities

- Ask students to construct a set of at least four computations, including one that is significantly different from the others.

- Name a number, and ask students to construct computations that give a result close to that number.

Odd Result Out

Which computational result doesn't seem to belong? Explain your reasoning.

1.

$9 \times 11 \times 24$	$25 \times 10 \times 10$
24×100	$99 \times 20 + 4$
80×30	$90 \times 30 - 300$

2.

$10 \times 10 \times 10$	2^{10}
32^2	$10 \times 10 \times 3$
4×256	8×128

3.

$50 \times 88 - 50 \times 40$	50×48
$25 \times 48 + 25 \times 48$	$100 \times 48 - 50 \times 48$
$48 \times 100 - 100$	49×51

Odd Result Out

Which computational result doesn't seem to belong? Explain your reasoning.

1.

$60 \times 50 \times 40$	100×120
$20 \times 60 \times 100$	$24 \times 50 \times 100$
$30 \times 40 \times 100$	2000×60

2.

$20 \times 50 \div \frac{1}{2}$	$20 \times 50 \times 2$
$(50 \div \frac{1}{2}) \times 20$	$(50 \div \frac{1}{2}) \times (20 \div \frac{1}{2})$
$50 \times 20 \div 0.5$	

3.

$\dfrac{40 \times 60 + 100}{20}$	$2400 \div 20 + 100 \div 20$
$20 \times 30 + 5$	$\dfrac{40 \times 60}{20} + \dfrac{10}{20}$
$2500 \div 20$	

What's Wrong Here?

Number Sense Focus

- Reasonableness
- Mental computation

Number Focus

- Activity 1: Whole numbers, fractions, decimals

Mathematical Background

Mathematical errors can often be detected by simple inspection or brief reflection. For example, the sum of two negative integers must be negative, a fact that makes sense in the physical world (if you have two debts, then you owe money; when calculating your net worth, the total amount of the debt would be represented by a negative sign). This idea must make sense in the symbolic world as well. The challenge for teachers is to help students appreciate the power of reflecting on their work.

Using the Activity

In this activity, students examine computations that contain at least one error.

1. As a warm-up, write a computation with an obvious error, such as $4 \times 25 = 105$, and ask what's wrong. Encourage students to explain their reasoning; for example:

   - "That's like four quarters, and four quarters is a dollar."

   - "I know 4 times 20 is 80 and 4 times 5 is 20, so it is 100."

   - "I know 4 times an odd number must be even, and 105 is odd."

2. Show the computations one at a time as the class discusses what is wrong in each and offers explanations of why the result is unreasonable.

Solutions

Given here are possible explanations for why each result is unreasonable.

Activity 1

1. Multiplying 2 and 5 already gives 10. Perhaps someone forgot to write the other zero.
2. Since $3 \times 4 = 12$, the power of 12 must be the same as the power of both 3 and 4.
3. The result must be larger because $150{,}000 \div 15 = 10{,}000$.
4. Since 4×250 is 1000, this result must be 10,000.
5. The product of four even numbers can't be odd.
6. Each fraction is greater than $\frac{1}{2}$ so the sum must be greater than 1.
7. There are eight $\frac{1}{4}$'s in 2, so $2 \div \frac{1}{4} = 8$.
8. Since $\frac{3}{4}$ is greater than $\frac{1}{2}$, the difference must be positive.
9. Three minus 1 is 2, so $3 - 1\frac{1}{4}$ must be less than 2.
10. $\frac{1}{5} + \frac{1}{5} = \frac{2}{5}$
11. The result must be positive.
12. The result must be negative, because ($^{-}$2) raised to the tenth power is positive, and a negative times a positive must be negative.
13. Since $8 - 2^3$ is zero, the product is 0.
14. Anything minus itself is 0.
15. ($^{-}$2) raised to the seventh power is negative, so the product must be negative.

Extending the Activity

• •

- Ask students to construct computations that contain an error and produce an unreasonable result. Have them post their computations on a bulletin board entitled *What's Wrong Here?*

- Ask students to review a previous assignment and search for an obvious error.

What's Wrong Here?

In each computation, how do you know that something is wrong?

1. $(2)(5)(10) = 10$

2. $3^2 \, 4^2 = 12^4$

3. $150{,}045 \div 15 = 103$

4. $250 \times 40 = 1000$

5. $2 \times 4 \times 6 \times 8 = 385$

6. $\dfrac{2}{3} + \dfrac{3}{4} = \dfrac{5}{7}$

7. $2 \div \dfrac{1}{4} = \dfrac{1}{2}$

8. $\dfrac{3}{4} - \dfrac{4}{8} = {}^-\dfrac{1}{4}$

9. $3 - 1\dfrac{1}{4} = 2\dfrac{3}{4}$

10. $\dfrac{1}{5} + \dfrac{1}{5} = \dfrac{2}{10}$

11. $^-5 - {}^-8 = {}^-3$

12. $^-3 \, (^-2)^{10} = 3072$

13. $15 \, (8 - 2^3) = 15$

14. $(^-5 - {}^-7) - (^-5 - {}^-7) = 4$

15. $(^-2)(^-2)(^-2)(^-2)(^-2)(^-2)(^-2) = 128$

EXPERIENCE 39

Where's the Point?

Number Sense Focus

- Reasonableness

Number Focus

- Activity 1: Decimals

Mathematical Background

The most frequent error made in operating with decimals is misplacement of the decimal point. Sometimes students spend more time recalling rules than thinking about the numbers and whether the answer is reasonable.

Using the Activities

In these activities, students are given computations with all the correct digits and challenged to use what they know about the numbers to correctly locate the decimal point in the results.

1. As a warm-up, set the stage with a story about a calculator that could calculate correctly but never displayed a decimal point. For example, if you computed 4.32×2.8, the calculator would report 12096. Ask students to explain where they think the decimal point belongs. Make a list of their explanations; for example:

   - "Count the number of decimal places from the right. That would be 2 plus 1, which is 3, so it goes between the 2 and 0."

   - "One factor is about 4 and the other is about 3, which makes the product about 12."

2. Reveal the computations one at a time, and invite students to decide whether a decimal point is needed to make the sentence reasonable and, if so, where it should be placed. Encourage students to share their explanations.

3. Make sure students observe that the last three results are the same. Ask them to discuss the relationships among the factors.

Solutions

Activity 1

1. 12.393
2. 23.60442
3. 177.98274
4. 26.74; This is one of several computations in which the counting rule does not work, because final zeros are not displayed.
5. 24.0269
6. 52.7978
7. 22.95
8. 97.0
9. 55.2
10. 80.
11. 6.35224
12. 63.5224
13. 635.224
14. 635.224
15. 635.224

Extending the Activities

• •

- Ask students for examples of real-world situations in which the product of two decimals is required.

Where's the Point?

The numbers in each result below are correct. Insert a decimal point in the result if it is needed to make the number sentence true.

1. $2.43 \times 5.1 = 12393$

2. $7.842 \times 3.01 = 2360442$

3. $8.97 \times 19.842 = 17798274$

4. $3.5 \times 7.64 = 2674$

5. $4.85 \times 4.954 = 240269$

6. $1.03 \times 51.26 = 527978$

7. $21.25 \times 1.08 = 2295$

8. $0.5 \times 194 = 970$

9. $0.25 \times 220.80 = 552$

10. $1.25 \times 64 = 80$

11. $4.688 \times 1.355 = 635224$

12. $46.88 \times 1.355 = 635224$

13. $4.688 \times 135.5 = 635224$

14. $46.88 \times 13.55 = 635224$

15. $468.8 \times 1.355 = 635224$

Number SENSE / Grades 6–8

Which Is the Best Estimate?

Number Sense Focus

- Reasonableness
- Mental computation

Number Focus

- Activities 1 and 3: Whole numbers, fractions
- Activity 2: Fractions, decimals

Mathematical Background

• •

Recognizing when different computations produce about the same results (such as 99^2 and 10^4), and when they produce unreasonable results, can be helpful for producing estimates, judging the relative size of results, and determining their reasonableness.

Using the Activities

• •

1. In each activity, show the computation to be estimated. Ask students which of the four possibilities produces an unreasonable answer. Encourage them to explain their thinking.

2. Ask students which method they prefer for estimating each computation, again sharing their reasoning.

Solutions

Activity 1

1. $\frac{50 \times 24}{20}$
2. $60 \times 100 \times 2$

Activity 2

1. $(0.19 + 0.34) \times (520 + 25)$
2. $0.5 \times 463 + 1300$

Activity 3

1. $120 + 4$
2. $\frac{45}{15} + \frac{240}{6}$

Extending the Activities

• •

- Ask students to construct a set of at least 4 computations that includes one that is significantly different from the others.

- Construct a multistep computation. Then ask students to make four computations that are close to the target and one that is not close. Ask them to tell why it is not close.

Which Is the Best Estimate?

1. To estimate this computation:

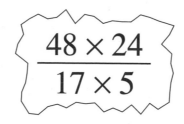

$$\frac{48 \times 24}{17 \times 5}$$

Here are four ways people have estimated.

$$\frac{50 \times 25}{100} \qquad \frac{51}{17} \times \frac{25}{5} \qquad \frac{50 \times 24}{20} \qquad 3 \times 5$$

Which produces an unreasonable answer? Why?

2. To estimate this computation:

$$0.24 \times 59 \times 0.891 \times 101$$

Here are four ways people have estimated.

$$60 \times \frac{1}{4} \times 90 \qquad 90 \times 15 \qquad 0.20 \times 60 \times 1 \times 100 \qquad 60 \times 100 \times 2$$

Which suggestion produces an unreasonable answer? Why?

Which Is the Best Estimate?

1. To estimate this computation:

$$0.19 \times 520 \times 0.34 \times 25$$

Here are four ways people have estimated.

$0.2 \times 500 \times 8$ $\qquad \dfrac{1}{5} \times 500 \times \dfrac{1}{3} \times 24$

$(0.19 + 0.34) \times (520 + 25)$ $\qquad 100 \times \dfrac{24}{3}$

Which suggestion produces an unreasonable answer? Why?

2. To estimate this computation:

$$0.945 \div 0.5034 \times 463 + 1283$$

Here are four ways people have estimated.

$0.5 \times 463 + 1300$ $\qquad\qquad 2 \times 460 + 1300$

$1300 + 900$ $\qquad\qquad\qquad 1 \times 2 \times 450 + 1300$

Which suggestion produces an unreasonable answer? Why?

Which Is the Best Estimate?

1. Suppose you wanted to estimate this computation:

$$0.736 \times 148 + 23 \div \frac{1}{6}$$

Which suggestion produces an unreasonable answer? Why?

$120 + 4$

$\frac{3}{4} \times 160 + 25 \times 5$

$120 + 20 \times 6$

$\frac{3}{4} \times 160 + 138$

2. Suppose you wanted to estimate this computation:

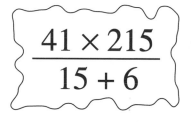

$$\frac{41 \times 215}{15 + 6}$$

Which suggestion produces an unreasonable answer? Why?

$\frac{45}{15} + \frac{240}{6}$

$\frac{40}{20} \times 200$

$\frac{30 \times 200}{20}$

$41 \times \frac{210}{21}$